1·50

To Gordon with Much Love from ... Hie

Medieval and Tu

Valerie E. Chancellor

Valerie E. Chancellor was educated at King Edward VI
High School for Girls, Birmingham, and at St Hugh's College,
Oxford, where she took a degree in Modern History. She has
had teaching experience both at girls' grammar schools and at
a Birmingham secondary modern school. She is now Senior
Lecturer in History at the West London Institute of Advanced
Education.

A History of Britain

Out of the Ancient World
Medieval and Tudor Britain
The Making of a Nation 1603–1789
Britain and the World 1789–1901
Britain in the Modern World: The Twentieth Century

Medieval and Tudor Britain

Valerie E. Chancellor

Penguin Books

Design: Arthur Lockwood

Illustration research: Naomi H. Jacoby

Penguin Books Ltd, Harmondsworth, Middlesex, England
Penguin Books, 625 Madison Avenue, New York, New York 10022, U.S.A.
Penguin Books Australia Ltd, Ringwood, Victoria, Australia
Penguin Books Canada Ltd, 2801 John Street, Markham, Ontario, Canada L3R 1B4
Penguin Books (N.Z.) Ltd, 182-190 Wairau Road, Auckland 10, New Zealand

First published 1967
Reprinted 1968, 1969, 1970, 1971, 1972, 1973, 1975 (twice), 1976, 1977, 1978, 1979

Copyright © Valerie E. Chancellor, 1967
All rights reserved

Printed in Hong Kong by Sheck Wah Tong Printing Press Ltd
Set in Lumitype Plantin

Contents

Chapter 1	Finding out about the Middle Ages	*page*	6
Chapter 2	Arthur and the coming of the Saxons		12
Chapter 3	Saint Augustine and the coming of Christianity		18
Chapter 4	Life in Saxon England		28
Chapter 5	Alfred and the Vikings		44
Chapter 6	Duke William and the Norman Conquest		50
Chapter 7	Thomas Becket and the struggle between Church and State		60
Chapter 8	Richard the Lion-heart and the Third Crusade		70
Chapter 9	An English traveller in the Middle Ages		78
Chapter 10	Edward I and the beginning of a united Britain		84
Chapter 11	Life in medieval England		94
Chapter 12	Joan of Arc and the Hundred Years War		120
Chapter 13	Wat Tyler and the Peasants' Revolt		128
Chapter 14	Wolsey and Cromwell – servants of a new monarchy		136
Chapter 15	Henry VIII – a Renaissance prince		148
Chapter 16	Archbishop Cranmer and the Reformation in England		158
Chapter 17	Queen Elizabeth I – a woman in power		168
Chapter 18	Life in Elizabethan England		178
Chapter 19	Gerard and Wentworth – Catholic and Puritan in the reign of Elizabeth		196
Chapter 20	Richard Hakluyt and the beginnings of the British Empire		204
	Index		214
	Acknowledgements		224

Chapter 1
Finding out about the Middle Ages

'I think of knights fighting battles, besieging forts and getting killed, and helping lovely ladies in distress.'

Like the boy who wrote those words about the Middle Ages, most of us have our own ideas about what they were really like. Perhaps they come from films or a TV series, from books or comics. It is much more difficult to see what those far off times have to do with us today.

What we owe to the Middle Ages

Yet if we look at the government of England, we find that in 1600 there was a monarch (a queen), a House of Commons and a House of Lords, just as there is now. Go further back to about the year A.D. 300 when we begin our story and you would find almost nothing like them. Obviously they must have grown up slowly during the Middle Ages. Again a modern farm may be quite different from a medieval manor, but it was the people of the manor who cleared away much of the dense forest that once covered large parts of England, and began to grow crops and tend animals there for the first time. The top photograph shows that we can sometimes see the outline of what was once a medieval village and its fields from the air. Many of our towns also grew up during the Middle Ages, and their narrow, winding streets cause some of our worst traffic jams.

How we know about the past

If we want to learn about the past, we have only to look around. The houses, churches, cathedrals and castles which were built in the Middle Ages not only tell us about the daily lives of the people, but set us thinking about the way their minds worked too. Why, for example, did they spend vast sums of money building large and beautiful churches and cathedrals when the homes even of rich people were dirty, cold and uncomfortable?

Another way to discover the Middle Ages is to dig in the earth. Much still lies buried in the state in which it was left so long ago. Sometimes there is real treasure, like a ship crammed with the riches of a Saxon prince which was found at Sutton Hoo. Each

Finding out by air photography. At Lower Ditchford, Gloucestershire, you can see traces of a medieval village, which the people left during the late fifteenth century when the land was turned over to sheep farming: mounds where houses stood; lines of streets; and the ridges and furrows of old ploughlands.

Tewkesbury today shows signs that it began during the Middle Ages: narrow, winding streets; a few half-timbered houses; and the abbey, which still dominates the town.

find is carefully described by the archaeologist and plans of the site where he has been digging are drawn.

Luckily the people of the Middle Ages have left us writings which also help us to understand them. Monks wrote about the past and kept records of what was going on in their own time. Some of these chroniclers, as they are called, clearly believed any story they heard. One of them tells us that in 1387 there was a talking head at Oxford which had the magic power of answering questions by nodding or shaking itself. How far can we believe a writer who passes on such a story? Also we must remember that the monks were keen supporters of the Church and praised its friends while being as rude as possible about its enemies. This means they would find little good to say about someone like King William Rufus, who made as much money as he could out of the

The Saxon ship discovered at Sutton Hoo in 1939. The timbers have rotted away, but their imprint and the nails which held them together remain. The ship was 80 feet long and 14 feet across at the widest part.

8

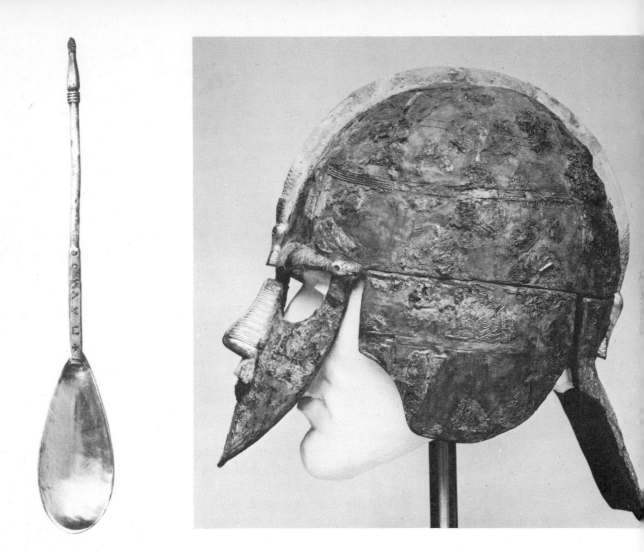

Sutton Hoo treasures. *Above:* silver spoon with 'Paul' written on the stem; *above right:* side view of a helmet made of sheet iron and decorated with silver and bronze; *right:* a purse-flap, decorated with gold, garnets and glass. They are now in the British Museum.

9

Church and once threatened to shake the saintly old Archbishop Anselm by the throat when he complained.

Other writings which tell us about the past are letters, sometimes from important people, but often from ordinary men and women to their friends. Also there are huge piles of documents kept by the king's servants. These include lists of cases tried in the law courts, of taxes paid or of people who did certain jobs. Most of these records are in Latin or in the sort of French spoken by William the Conqueror, but not spoken in France today. Few people can read them easily now, for medieval handwriting is different from ours.

In this book quotations from writers of the past have nearly all been put into modern English. As you work from them and the drawings, and study the illustrations, which are of manuscripts, books and objects from the period being described, you may feel something of the excitement of finding out about the past for yourselves.

Things to do

1   Make a list of all the books, comics, films or TV plays dealing with the Middle Ages which you have read or seen. Which of them gave you the clearest picture of life in those times?
2   Look at the pictures of the Sutton Hoo ship burial and describe one of the finds in detail, as an archaeologist would do. Most of the things which the prince would need in the next life were there, but his body was missing. Can you think why?
3   Opposite is an alphabet written in Tudor times. First write your name and then a sentence or two about the Middle Ages using this sort of writing.
4   A monk wrote this about King William Rufus. Read it through and answer the questions underneath.

While Lanfranc was alive, William showed a horror of evil so that some people hoped he would be a good example to other kings. Later, where he had been generous, he grew wasteful; where he had been strict, he grew cruel. He feared God too little and man not at all . . . . In his time the fashion of flowing hair, fanciness in dress and shoes with curved points came in.

(a) What have you read in the chapter to make you think that the monk writing may not have been fair to the king?
(b) What sort of character did King William Rufus have?

(c) What tells you that Archbishop Lanfranc must have been a powerful man?

(d) What were the new fashions of King William Rufus' time? Do you think the monk approved or not?

Book to read

G. Grigson, *Looking and Finding*, Phoenix House

A sixteenth-century copy book. There are two kinds of 's': one for use in the middle of the word, the other at the end. There are no 'j's: 'i's were used instead.

Chapter 2
Arthur and the coming of the Saxons

'Hear the groans of the Britons! The barbarians drive us into the sea and the sea drives us back to the barbarians. Our only choice is whether to be drowned or murdered.'

This cry for help to a leading Roman general, Aetius, in the year A.D. 446 brought no reply. The Romans were too busy fighting off their enemies elsewhere to bother about the small island of Britain which was almost completely cut off from the rest of Europe.

The end of Roman rule

The 'barbarians' – so called because of their wildness and cruelty – were drawn to the Roman empire by its wealth. These hungry, wandering people wanted not only its gold and silver, but also its land so that they could grow food. At the same time the Roman emperors were losing their grip on the vast lands which they ruled. They tried to solve the problem by dividing the empire into two more manageable halves. Byzantium (Constantinople) became the capital in the East, as shown on the map opposite. The Roman emperors were still short of money and troops, however. Heavy taxation had weakened trade and the towns which depended on it. Even such money as was collected in taxes was often stolen by dishonest officials before it could be used to pay the armies which defended the boundaries of the empire. Also the life of an emperor tended to be short and he was often murdered by a rival for power. For example, Aetius, to whom the Britons sent the letter asking for help, was killed on the orders of an emperor who was jealous of his success. Aetius' friends then murdered the emperor.

In such troubled times, therefore, the Britons had to struggle on by themselves. For years they had faced the attacks of Scots and Picts in the north and west. Now new dangers began to threaten them. A strange plague swept across the land. Those who lived through it found themselves starving as the harvest failed and gangs of desperate peasants roamed around stealing and killing. Worst of all, the barbarians began to arrive from Germany.

Statue of a Roman legionary found in Yorkshire.

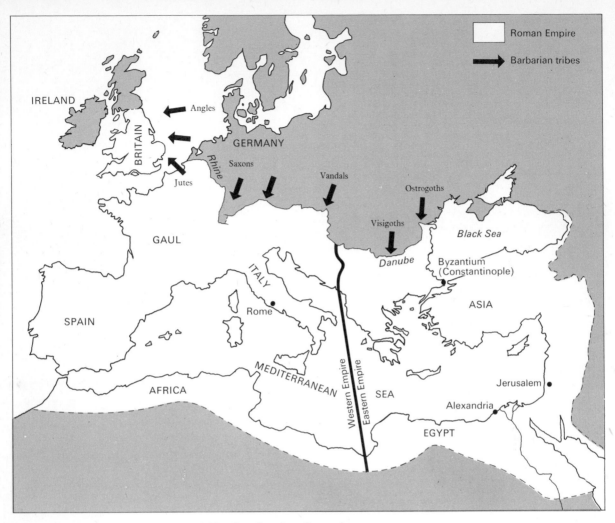

Map legend:
- Roman Empire
- Barbarian tribes

Labels on map: IRELAND, BRITAIN, GERMANY, Angles, Saxons, Rhine, Jutes, GAUL, Vandals, Ostrogoths, Visigoths, Black Sea, Danube, Byzantium (Constantinople), SPAIN, ITALY, Rome, ASIA, Western Empire, Eastern Empire, MEDITERRANEAN, SEA, AFRICA, Jerusalem, Alexandria, EGYPT

Barbarians invade the
Holy Roman Empire.

The barbarian invasions

The first invaders, led by Hengist, are said to have been invited
by the ruler, Vortigern, who needed their help against other
British princes. Once they landed these tall, blond warriors quickly
took over the whole of Kent. They sent back to Germany news of
the country and its people who had grown soft with the comforts
of Roman rule. Large armies of barbarians set out to brave the
storms of the North Sea in their frail ships. We can trace the way
they went after arriving in Britain because they burnt or cremated
their dead instead of burying them like the Christian Britons. The
ashes from Saxon cremations lie along the banks of big rivers,
such as the Thames, and on routes like the Icknield Way which
link rivers together. You can see from the map on the next page
how the Jutes, Angles and Saxons shared England between them.

13

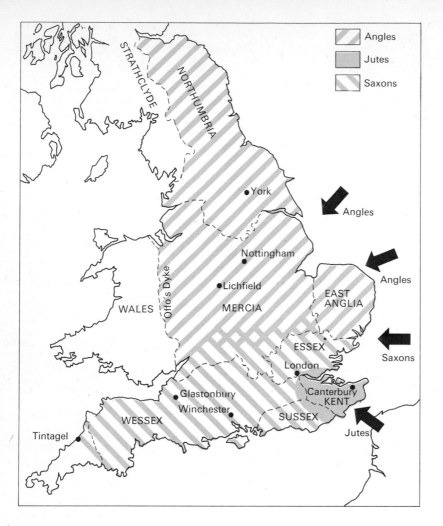

Barbarians in Britain.

The Britons suffered terribly. Rich and poor alike were caught and made into slaves or butchered on the spot. The dead were left to rot because none of their friends was left to bury them. Those who escaped fled west and hid themselves in mountain and forest country where many of them died for lack of food.

The British revival

One Briton at least did not give in without a fight. The warrior Arthur and his men made one last desperate stand. The ditches and walls of the hill forts were repaired and at Mount Badon the enemy was crushed and thrown back. We know very little about Arthur and his battles. His name means a bear, which perhaps gives us a clue to what he looked like. He may have commanded a force of cavalry which could move quickly to deal with any new

A hill fort in Cornwall, with a circular ditch. It dates from the Iron Age.

danger. The barbarians, who rode to the battlefield but dismounted to fight, were not used to meeting an enemy on horseback. The sight of Arthur and his knights riding into battle may have frightened even the Saxons.

His run of success lasted for twenty years and we are not sure how or why it ended. Perhaps Arthur was killed by a blow from a Saxon sword or spear, or perhaps he just became old and tired fighting for a people who had grown soft under the peaceful rule of the Romans and did little to defend themselves. This story, which was told by the Welsh and written down by Geoffrey of Monmouth hundreds of years later, is as likely to be true as any other. In it Arthur fights Medrod, a Briton who has betrayed him.

Medrod waited for Arthur by the river Camlann with an army of 60,606 men. He promised his followers all the land and treasure they wanted. Arthur told his men, 'These foreign-tongued people will never fight well together, for they lack the courage of us Christians. We are in the right and they are in the wrong.' The fighting was so fierce that the cries and screams of the wounded nearly drove them mad. Towards evening Arthur fell upon Medrod's army and tore it apart as a lion scatters tame animals. He killed Medrod and thousands with him. And there also Arthur was wounded unto death and they carried him away from the battlefield.

After Arthur's death the Saxons had more success. The Britons were pushed back into Wales, Devon, Cornwall, and the wooded land north of the Thames. There they kept to their own language and customs. In their stories Arthur became a king with a beautiful queen named Guinevere and followers such as Lancelot and Gawain who met with him at a round table.

A new nation

As you can see from the map, the coming of the barbarians meant that Britain was a divided land. It was only slowly during the Middle Ages that the different races learnt to live together in peace and to form one nation. It was some time also before trade and travel between England and Europe revived. The skills which had sometimes brought comfort and cleanliness to the towns and villas of the Britons had vanished. Only in a few parts of western Britain and in Ireland did the art, learning and religion of the Roman empire survive. Britain had become an isolated and barbarian land.

The earliest mention of King Arthur is in the *Annales Cambriae* (Annals of Wales, late tenth century): 'The battle of Camlann in which Arthur and Medraut (Medrod) fell.'

Dates to remember

446 British appeal to Aetius for help
about 500 Arthur's victory at Mount Badon

Things to do

1 Study the story of Arthur's death carefully. Can you find any places where the writer is not telling the truth or exaggerating what happened? What does Arthur say before the battle which leads you to think that Medrod is fighting with the help of the Saxons?
2 Pretend you are one of Arthur's knights. Describe how the Saxons came to Britain and how you fought them.

16

3 Place names tell us a lot, e.g., Essex is the land of the East Saxons and Northumbria is the land north of the Humber. Guess which people lived in these areas:
(a) Sussex   (b) Wessex   (c) Middlesex   (d) East Anglia.
4 The Saxons settled in places which often have 'ton' (town), 'ham' (homestead or village), or 'ing' (family or tribe) in their names. See how many of these place-names you can collect.

Book to read

B. Kennedy Cooke, *King Arthur of Britain*, Edmund Ward

Legends of Arthur grew up during the Middle Ages (especially in France where this painting comes from) in which he was said to be the leader of the knights of Christian Europe, whom he seated at a round table.

Chapter 3
Saint Augustine and the coming of Christianity

Pagan England

We do not know when or where the Christian faith at last died out in those parts of England where the Saxons settled. One by one the altar lamps went out. The last Christian died or gave up his religion. Soon even the church buildings crumbled away.

The invaders worshipped Woden, King of the Gods; Queen Frig, the Mother Goddess; Tiw, the violent God of War, and Thunor, the fierce Thunder God. All these were known in Germany too, but there were one or two gods, such as Eostre and Hretha, which only the English worshipped. They have given their names to Easter and the earth. The worship of the gods was led by priests who were forbidden to fight or carry weapons. They held services before idols which stood in holy places, often on the top of hills where they could be seen for miles around. All the idols were destroyed when England became a Christian country and since they were made of wood, which burns and rots easily, no traces of them have been found. Probably they looked something like an Indian totem pole.

Augustine's mission

It was not the Britons but Pope Gregory the Great who first saw the need to bring Christianity to the Saxons. It is said that he saw a group of fair-haired boys being sold in the market at Rome. He was told that they were Angles from Britain. Gregory replied that 'Angles' was a good word for them because they looked like angels. It became one of his aims to see that the Angles were given the chance to become angels by being converted to Christianity.

For this task he chose Augustine, a monk, and sent him off with a few followers. Within a short time Augustine returned. He had heard stories in France about the savagery of the Saxons and was in a panic at the thought of meeting them when he did not even know their language. Gregory soothed his fears and Augustine set out once more. He found interpreters in France and landed on the isle of Thanet in Kent in the year 596.

The king, Ethelbert, already had a Christian wife, Bertha, who was a Frankish princess. In spite of this he did not invite

St Martin's Church, Canterbury, probably the earliest existing church in England. It was built by King Ethelbert for Queen Bertha, and St Augustine arrived there with his followers in 597. Ethelbert is supposed to have been baptized at it in the same year. The church has been much restored since.

Augustine to cross to the mainland, and would only meet him in the open air so that the stranger's magic would not get a chance to work on him. The monks approached Ethelbert with a silver cross and a picture of Jesus carried before them. After a hymn and prayer, Augustine spoke to the pagans. The king did not feel able to give up his old beliefs, but he allowed the monks to settle in the town of Canterbury and to try to convert the people. Later he became so impressed with Augustine's holy way of life that he was baptized along with many of his leading men. His nephew, Sabert, who ruled Essex, was also converted.

The Celtic Christians

Augustine then tried to arrange a meeting with the leaders of the British Church. The people of Wales, western Britain and Ireland had remained true to their faith, although the coming of the Saxons had cut them off from all contact with the Pope in Rome. They kept Easter on a different date from the Roman Christians and saw no reason why they should obey Gregory. Some of them, such as St David and St Columba, were very holy men. They believed that suffering would bring them nearer to God and prayed for hours, standing up to their necks in icy water, or wore

rough hair shirts full of lice. Sometimes they claimed strange powers over birds and animals.

At last seven Celtic bishops agreed to meet Augustine and to accept him as their archbishop if he seemed meek and saintly. Unfortunately, he showed his bad manners by not getting up to greet them as they approached. They took offence and refused to obey Augustine or his master, the Pope. Over half a century was to pass before the Celtic church gave up its independence.

The King of Northumbria decided to bring back the Christian faith which had died out in his lands. He invited the Celtic monk, Aidan, to come from the Scottish island of Iona and convert his people. From his headquarters on Lindisfarne, Aidan and his followers spread the Christian faith throughout Lindsay, the land of the Middle Angles, Essex, and Mercia, the most firmly pagan of all the Saxon kingdoms. The Christians of Kent had no part in all this missionary work, but the King of Northumbria had married a Kentish wife. They quarrelled over what was the right date for Easter and at last a synod, or meeting, of the church was held at Whitby in 664. After hearing arguments on both sides, King Oswy decided in favour of obeying the Pope, the successor of St Peter.

'Do you both agree,' the king went on, 'that our Lord was speaking to Peter and that he gave him the keys of heaven?' The speakers for both sides answered, 'We do.' Then the king said 'I tell you St Peter is the keeper of the gates of heaven and I shall not set myself against him. I shall obey him in every way in case, when I come to heaven, he who holds the keys may not unlock the gates for me.'

So the work of Augustine was at last complete. The Archbishop

The monastery on the island of Iona today. No traces of the original wooden church and huts have survived. The monastery was founded by St Columba, a Celt, who wanted to convert the Picts.

of Canterbury became the leader of a united Church in England, though his power was sometimes challenged later by the Archbishop of York.

The Church in England

During the coming centuries England was divided up into dioceses each ruled by a bishop. The diocese was then divided into parishes, each in the charge of a priest. The man of medieval times came into contact with the Church at every point in his life. As a baby he was baptized. Often the only teaching a child received was from the priest who preached at the Mass on Sundays. When he grew up and was confirmed into the Church by his bishop, he was supposed to confess all his sins to the priest who would give him

Celtic crosses, recognizable by the circle which surrounds the two arms of the cross and by the patterns carved on them. *Below left:* part of one from the island of Lindisfarne; *right:* from Ireland. Both are eighth century.

penances – that is, things to do as a sign that he was sorry for the wrongs he had done. When he married, it was usually with the blessing of the Church. His holidays were religious feast days and on fast days he would go without food like everyone else. To be cut off from the services of the Church and the company of Christian people by excommunication seemed a terrible punishment to all but the most hardened sinner. As he lay dying, he would make his confession and receive the Last Sacrament in the hope that his time in purgatory would be short. There, he believed, he would undergo punishment which would cleanse him of his sins so that he could enter heaven. Only those beyond hope went to hell.

The monasteries

Some people found it hard to live a Christian life amid the cares and temptations of a savage world. Instead they chose to live in monasteries or convents with other religious people.

In early Christian times men and women had settled in deserted places so that they could worship God in peace. One of these, St Benedict, drew up a set of rules for his followers at Monte Cassino in Italy. Most of the monks and nuns of the Middle Ages, including Augustine, also tried to obey them.

Anyone who wanted to become a monk had first to spend a trial period as a novice before he could take his final vows and leave the world for ever. The promises he would make were not the same in all monasteries, but were usually something like this:

I, . . . , here give up my parents, my brothers and relatives, everything I own, and the worthless glory and pleasure of this world. I also give up my own will and put the will of God in its place. I accept all the hardship of a monk's life, and take the vows of poverty, chastity and obedience in the hope of heaven; and I promise to remain a monk in this monastery all the days of my life.

A monk's life

Life in the monastery was not easy. The monk was allowed to keep nothing that he could call his own. Even his coarse robe and sandals, his handkerchief, pen and knife were the same as those given to everyone else by the monks in charge of supplies. Twice a day he had a good meal, though it was not supposed to include meat. Discipline was very strict. Sins, such as quarrelling or falling asleep in the services, had to be confessed to the other monks. Punishments included whipping, fasting and lying on the

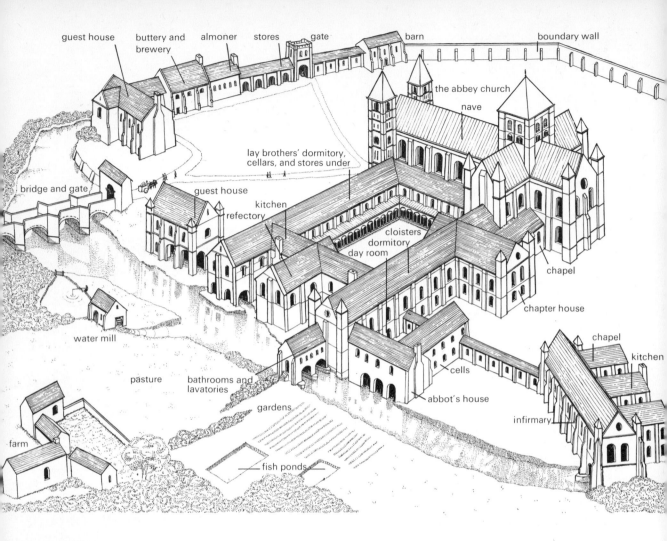

Drawing of a monastery.

Abbey church   Services were held at 2 a.m., sunrise, 11 a.m., 12.30 p.m., 6 p.m., and sunset.

Cloisters   Here the novices (young boys who hoped to become monks) played or studied, while the older monks copied manuscripts.

Dormitory   Monks went to bed at sunset, but rose at 2 a.m. for the night service.

Lay brothers' dormitory   The lay brothers, who lived here, helped in the monastery and attended services, but were not monks.

Cellars and stores   Drink and food were kept here and in the **buttery and brewery.**

Refectory   Meals were at midday and at about 7 p.m. One of the monks read from the Bible while the others ate.

Chapter house   The monks held a meeting here at about 7 a.m. each day, led by the abbot or his second in command, the prior.

Infirmary   Here the sick were looked after.

Bathrooms and lavatories   Sanitation in monasteries was much better than elsewhere in the country.

Guest houses   There were few inns outside the towns and monasteries acted as hotels for travellers.

Almoner's house   It was the almoner's duty to give gifts of food and clothing to the poor.

incipit euangelii
genelogia mathei

Liber

generationis

iesu xpi filii dauid filii abraham

floor at the entrance to the chapel so that the other brothers might walk over the sinner as they entered. Long periods were spent in silence and even commands which seemed impossible had to be obeyed. A monk might leave the monastery only when he went on an errand for the abbot. When he died, he would be buried in the monastery grounds.

St Benedict believed that 'Idleness is the enemy of the soul', and 'To work is to pray', so every moment of a Benedictine monk's life was busy. Eight times a day he went to worship in the church. The rest of his time was spent in study or in work about the monastery or the fields. Everyone had to take a turn at the harder tasks, such as digging, scrubbing floors or washing up. Some of the monks looked after the infirmary or hospital ward. There, poor people or travellers who had been taken ill could be treated as well as sick monks. The one at Fountains Abbey in Yorkshire was very large, and from its windows patients could hear the soothing sound of a nearby stream. The more learned monks spent their time in copying and decorating manuscripts, writing, and teaching the young. Some children were sent to the monastery to be educated and many stayed on to become monks.

In this way the ancient learning of Greece and Rome was preserved and passed on to the young. In Saxon times the finest artists and scholars were nearly all monks. Caedmon, one of the first English poets, lived in the monastery at Whitby. The historian, Bede, who was probably born in A.D. 673, wrote down most of what we know about the conversion of England. He got his facts not only from talking to people but also from the manuscripts and letters in the fine libraries of the monasteries at Wearmouth and Jarrow where he worked.

A monk at his writing-desk. He holds a knife to sharpen his quill pen.

Left: a page from the Lindisfarne gospels, written in Northumbria in the seventh century. *Right:* detail of an initial letter, decorated with animal heads. Compare with the decoration on the Celtic crosses, page 21.

A Christian nation

Few Saxons would know or care that the Church was saving the learning of the past and bringing England back into touch with Europe. Bede gives us some idea of what the coming of Christianity meant to the pagan English at the time. He says that the high priest of Northumbria, Coifi, gave this description of his faith to the king:

The life of man . . . seems to me like a single sparrow flying through the Hall where you sit in winter to feast with your noblemen and advisers. Inside there is a warm fire, but outside a wintry storm of snow and rain rages. The sparrow flies swiftly in through one door of the Hall and out through the other. Inside he is safe, but he soon vanishes again into the darkness. In the same way man dwells on earth for a little while, but he knows nothing of what went before or will come after.

The Christians of the Middle Ages never felt this doubt. They were sure that heaven, hell or purgatory awaited them after death. Their life on earth was a testing time to see which one it was to be.

Dates to remember

528   St Benedict settled at Monte Cassino
596   Augustine reached Kent
664   The synod of Whitby

Things to do

1   Find out which days of the week are named after Saxon gods. Some place names also show that pagan worship took place there. Look in an atlas for places where Woden or Thunor were worshipped, e.g., Wednesbury and Thursley.
2   Write a conversation between a pagan Saxon and a Christian of the Middle Ages in which they compare their beliefs.
3   From the map on page 27 make a list of the different English kingdoms and say whether they were converted by Roman or Celtic Christians.
4   Study the drawing of a monastery. Then imagine that you have been taken on a conducted tour of such a monastery and describe what you would see.
5   Start to keep a notebook of the lives of famous people. Using the list of books on page 27 as a guide, find out all you can

A crozier (or staff) of the eighth century from the monastery of Kells, Ireland.

about Gregory the Great, St David, St Patrick, St Columba, St Cuthbert, St Aidan and St Benedict.

Books to read

D. Leatham, *The Church Defies the Dark Ages*, Religious Education Press

H. R. E. Davidson, *The Golden Age of Northumbria*, Longman

R. J. Unstead, *Monasteries*, Black

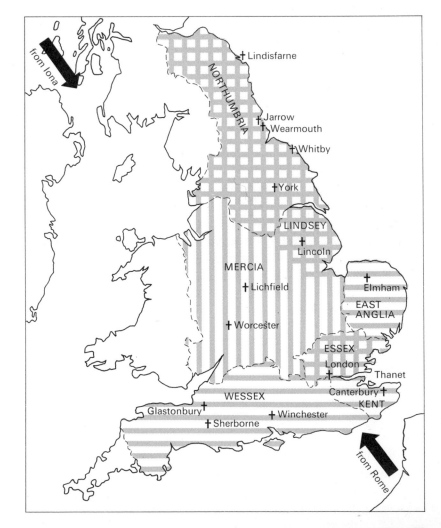

lands converted by Roman missionaries

lands converted by Celtic missionaries

lands converted first by Roman and then by Celtic missionaries

✝ centres of Christianity

The conversion of England. Ireland was converted by St Patrick in the fifth century and remained devout Christians.

Chapter 4
Life in Saxon England

The land

When they stepped ashore, the Saxons found a Britain very different from what we know today. As you may remember from *A History of Britain* SH1, the Britons farmed mostly in the light, chalky soil to be found on Salisbury Plain and other areas of the south. Dense forest and marshland covered much of the rest of the country. Even the fertile soil along the river valleys was generally left unfarmed until the Saxons arrived with a new and stronger type of plough which could turn over heavy ground.

Loyalty to a lord

Like the Americans who moved into the Wild West, the Saxons were pioneers in a land of hostile natives, and rugged country which had been untouched by man. Because they felt themselves surrounded by danger and difficulty, they saw the need to stick together. Each man followed a lord whom he vowed to defend to the death. In return he received his lord's protection at all times together with gifts of weapons and treasure, if his lord was successful in battle.

The Saxons enjoyed stories of warriors who had fought on when a battle was lost to avenge their lord or to die with him. Bede tells us of Lilla, a follower of King Edwin of Northumbria, who was stabbed and killed as he threw himself between his lord and the enemy who had come to murder him. A famous Saxon poem gives us a picture of the man whose lord is dead:

> Even in sleeping the sorrow comes on him,
> And dreaming he clutches his dear lord once more . . .
> Then from his sleep he awakes on his own,
> Seeing grey billows of sea spread before him,
> Sea-birds dipping with out-stretched wings,
> While hail, snow, drive forth from the lowering skies.

A king and his people

A king was the greatest of the lords in his kingdom but he was not all-powerful. Below him came the ealdormenn and thanes, who with the bishops made up the king's Witan, a council of wise

A Saxon woman appeals to the king for justice.

o rud dæle. ꝑþu nðde æl þeodig onþain eaꝇðe
ꝼe ðct heo ꝑaþe hyr ſꝑuꝛtoꞃ: þaꞃ lnðe
nɪnɡ tõ. ꞃ hꞇ nyman þꞃiꞅ꞉ ꞅoꞃ hyꞃe ꝓlutetõhꝛ

men. This advised the king and sometimes even decided who should be next on the throne, if there was any doubt.

A Saxon king and his Witan have reached a verdict.

It was the custom for the king and his court to travel round the country to each of his estates or farms in turn. He would stay there until food and other supplies ran out and then move on again. His chief duties were to protect his subjects in case of war, to keep the peace and see that justice was done. In return he demanded taxes paid in farm produce or money. He also expected every able-bodied freeman to fight for him in the fyrd (army).

There were many of these freemen or churls, as they were called, in Saxon England. They were given land and stock such as corn and cattle from their lord and in return they worked for him for two days a week or more when needed. They paid rent in money or in grain or livestock, such as hens, pigs and cows. However hard their life might be, they did at least know that they were free and could leave for another part of the country and another lord if they wished. Few of them ever did this because it would mean too much change and hardship for their families.

In contrast the slaves of Saxon England had no escape. They were owned by their masters, who even had the right to kill them if they wanted. The murderer of a slave was punished not for taking life, but for doing damage to another man's property.

Justice and the law

Except for the slave, every man had his wergild, or blood price, which was paid by a murderer as compensation to the family of the murdered man. It might cost 1200 shillings to kill a thane, but only 200 shillings to kill an ordinary churl. Even parts of the body came to have their wergilds. An eye or right arm (with which a warrior held his sword) were valued more highly than an ear or a toe, for example. A nose was worth sixty shillings, a fore-finger fifteen shillings and its nail only four shillings.

Before there were laws which fixed wergilds, each man had avenged an injury to himself and his family. This led to blood feuds between families which might go on for years. Saxon kings seem to have found fines a better way than the death penalty to stop this wasteful warfare. Still a man could be hanged or beheaded for such crimes as the theft of cattle or goods, fire-raising, or treachery to the king. More often he was whipped or had an arm or foot cut off. The Saxons seem to have felt that there was usually some doubt about a man's guilt except when he was caught red-handed. So they usually spared a criminal's life.

There was no police force to catch a suspect and a man or woman might be accused on suspicion rather than because there was any proof of guilt. The ealdormann or his sheriff would be in charge of the trial and could offer the accused two ways of proving his innocence. One way was to get men of good character to swear that he was innocent. The other was to undergo trial by ordeal. A priest would command the accused to confess if he was guilty. Then he would be given holy water to drink and thrown into a pond or stream. If he floated, he was held to be guilty,

Whipping a Saxon. The man on the right is heating a branding-iron which will mark the wrong-doer for life.

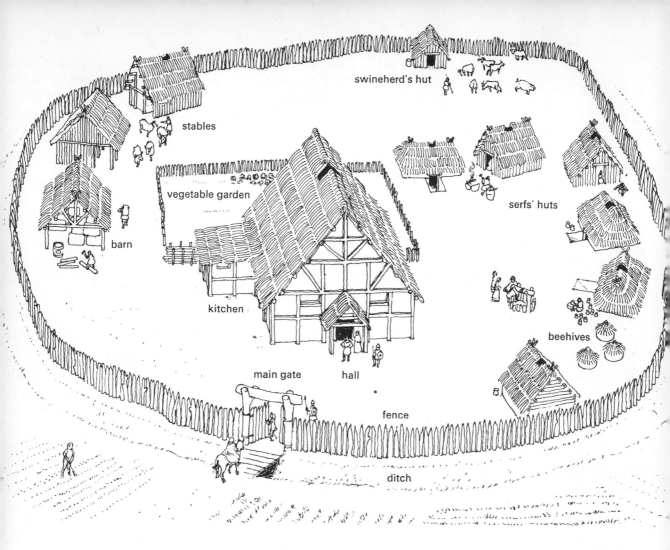

swineherd's hut

stables

vegetable garden

serfs' huts

barn

kitchen

beehives

main gate

hall

fence

ditch

for it was thought that water was so pure that it would only receive an innocent man. Other ordeals were to carry a red-hot iron for ten feet, or to plunge a hand into boiling water and bring out a stone. If the accused's burns showed signs of healing without going septic within three days, the priest would declare him innocent. Fire was supposed to harm the guilty man more than the innocent.

The village settlement

One of the reasons why it was so hard to keep law and order in Saxon times was the difficulty of getting from one place to another along the remains of Roman roads or the faint tracks worn by other travellers. This also meant that each village had to be self-supporting. Its people could never count on visits from pedlars.

A Saxon village settlement. The fence and ditch protected it from being raided.

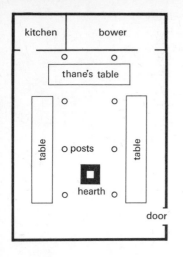

Plan of a Saxon hall.

Look at the drawing of a Saxon settlement. You will see that the hall is the most important building. It was there that the thane, his family and servants would live. Inside there was a fireplace in the centre of the main room, with long tables on either side. The lord and his guests sat at a table which ran across one end of the hall. The Saxons enjoyed drinking mead, a drink made from honey, and feasting on bread, roast meats, and vegetables such as leeks, onions and beans. During the feast there might be entertainment from a minstrel who would play the harp and sing, perhaps about Beowulf, the great warrior who was said to have died from wounds received in a battle against a dragon, the guardian of a great treasure:

> The monstrous dragon, enraged by the fight
> Lunged at the King when he got the chance,
> With fiery flame he buried his fangs
> In Beowulf's throat; he was spattered in blood
> As his life streamed out from the gory wound.

At night the trestle tables would be taken down so that guests could lie down to sleep among the rushes on the hall floor. Others went off to the living rooms (or 'bowers') nearby where they could enjoy greater comfort and privacy.

A lord and his lady

At dawn the lord might rise and spend the day in hunting, or fighting, or seeing that the law was obeyed, or just looking over the settlement to see that all was going well. His wife stayed at home looking after her children and giving the servants their

Hunting wild boar.

Saxon women wind and weave wool. Underneath are scenes of hell.

orders. Sometimes she would join the other women in spinning wool or flax into thread and weaving it into cloth for clothes like the ones you see in the picture. She also supervised the making of bread, butter and cheese and the brewing of mead. Often she looked after the sick and taught some of the local children. Saxon women were usually quite well treated. There was even a law that they should not be forced to marry if they did not want to, though if a suitor offered a good price for her, it was hard for a girl to go against her father's wishes and refuse him. One Saxon poem tells of a wife whose marriage had been happy, but whose husband had turned against her:

> Happily once we often boasted
> That only death should drive us apart.
> All that is gone and our love of old . . .
> The hate of my love follows me fast.

A churl's life

Life was hard for both men and women who were churls and slaves. They lived in the hall or in dirty, overcrowded huts near

Above: model of a seventh-
century weaver's hut. Huts
were dug into the ground and
covered with a thatched roof.

Right: a group of Saxon
peasants.

the hall. Some of the churls had special jobs such as looking after the bees or pigs. Others did the work needed at each season of the year on their own and the lord's land. Spring ploughing and sowing was followed by hay-making in the summer and harvesting in the autumn. Then those animals which were not to be kept for breeding were slaughtered and the meat salted so that it lasted through the winter. Finally, ploughing began again as the winter came on.

One writer tells us of a typical day in a churl's life:

I go out at dawn, driving the oxen to the field, and yoke them to the plough. It is never so harsh a winter that I dare stay at home for fear of my master, but when the oxen have been yoked and the plough-share and coulter fastened to the plough, I must plough a full acre or more each day . . . I have to fill the oxen's manger with hay and clear out the dung.

For the Saxon peasant, life was one long battle against starvation. If the crops failed or the animals died, there was no hope of importing more from abroad. Englishmen have always moaned about the weather, and in the work of Saxon writers we often hear about bitter cold, hail, rain, snow and high winds. This sort of weather meant not only that the people in their flimsy clothes and homes suffered from the chill and damp, but also that they and their children might well die from lack of food.

The three fields

Outside the village settlement, but adjoining it, there were three large fields, each divided up into strips by ditches and banks. In one field barley or wheat grew; in another, oats, while the third was left fallow with nothing growing in it at all. The most important men in the village were given most strips, but even the humblest churls could expect strips in each of the three fields so that they would be sure of having two crops to gather in at harvest-time.

The Saxons knew little about manures and fertilizers, but they did find out that unless a field was allowed to lie fallow every three years so that the ground was rested, it would grow poor, sparse crops. Apart from this, they depended on magic spells and prayers to make their land fruitful. Sometimes they left an offering of a loaf sprinkled with milk and holy water where the first furrow was ploughed.

Towns and trade

Most Saxons lived in village settlements, for there were very few

Ploughing in January. A companion scatters seed upon the furrows.

Breaking up the soil in March, digging, sowing and raking in the seed.

Harvesting in August, with sickles and shears. Only the top of the corn is cut. It is then thrown to the man with the pitchfork beside the cart.

Threshing and winnowing in December. Chaff and grain are separated by beating and sieving. All four illustrations are from an old English calendar of the eleventh century.

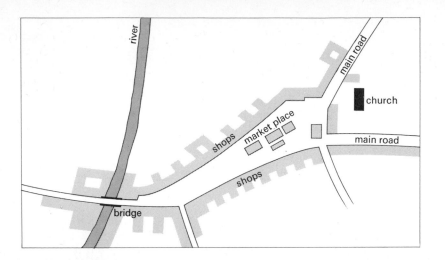

Plan of a Saxon town.

A Saxon church at Bradford-on-Avon, Wiltshire, with small, rounded, typically Saxon arches.

Jewellery. *Above:* a bronze belt-clasp from fifth-century Kent; *below:* a seventh-century ring from Suffolk; *right:* a seventh-century necklace of gold and garnets from Northamptonshire.

towns. During the barbarian invasions trade in Western Europe had nearly died out. Money was rarely used. Instead, local traders exchanged or bartered one lot of goods for another. As the invaders settled down, and became more peaceful, trade in such goods as salt, iron, fish and lead, which were found only in certain parts of the country, started up again.

The Saxons avoided the old Roman towns at first, for they seem to have thought that ghosts haunted the ruins. However, they later began to settle in or near them, for they had been founded at places which were easy for merchants to reach, such as cross-roads, or near a ford over a river, or at a good harbour. The biggest towns in Saxon England included London, York, Winchester, Lincoln, Canterbury and Oxford. By the tenth century they had between five to ten thousand inhabitants who were crammed into the small tenements which bordered their streets.

Most trade was still done locally in such goods as cloth and jewellery which the townsmen sold to people in the outlying settlements in exchange for food. Some goods, however, did reach Britain from further east, coming through France. They included silks, spices, wine, oil, ivory, brass and glass. In return the English exported wool, cloth and cheese. There was also a

A fishing-boat, taking a monk to the island of Crowland in the Lincolnshire marshes. There seems to be little leg-room, and no protection against the wind.

A glass vase, imported from the Continent. It was found in Kent, which kept in touch with other European countries in early Saxon times.

trade in slaves who were sold to work for masters in other countries.

Saxon England and the world

The Saxons lived on the edge of the known world of their time. To the west lay only the sea, for as yet the American lands beyond it were unknown. To the east the Saxons traded with most of the people of Western Europe. Their kings sometimes made treaties with great rulers such as Charles the Great whose Holy Roman Empire included France, Germany and Italy. We hear of Saxons who journeyed to Rome to visit the Pope and to Jerusalem to see the places where Jesus lived. To the north they had many links with the Scandinavian countries, especially after the Danes began to settle in England.

Although it was such a small, remote country, England won fame as a centre of learning and Christianity. When others had given up hope of ever converting the fierce, pagan tribes of Germany, it was a group of Saxon missionaries led by St Boniface

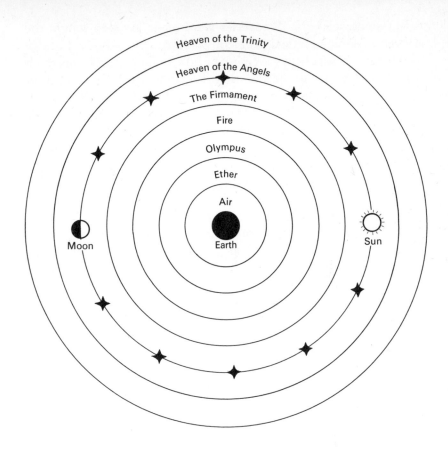

Heaven of the Trinity
Heaven of the Angels
The Firmament
Fire
Olympus
Ether
Air
Earth
Moon
Sun

The universe as Bede believed it to be.

who at last succeeded in making them Christian. So famous were English scholars that when Charles the Great wanted to begin a school at his palace in 782, he sent for the Saxon teacher Alcuin to take charge of it. English manuscripts like the one you see on page 24 were prized all over Europe. Even today Bede is still thought to be one of the greatest historians, and all later writers in Europe have followed his example in dating events from the birth of Jesus.

The beginnings of science

Bede's work was also important because he studied Greek and Roman ideas about the world and its place in the universe. These he passed on to his readers. He believed that the earth was fixed motionless in space and encased in seven heavens, as you can see from the diagram. For centuries no one doubted that Bede was right, for only the monks had much time to spare from the hard tasks of everyday life and they usually chose to spend it in thinking about God rather than His creation.

Yet some scientific discoveries were made. As men sought the answer to some practical problem, such as how to build a bridge which would bear heavy weights or how to forge a weapon which would not break in battle, they added to their knowledge of physics and chemistry almost without knowing it. When the Saxon doctor, Bald, noted down the symptoms of smallpox or the common cold or described how he had set a broken bone or amputated a limb, he added a few facts to medical knowledge which others might build on in the future. For centuries patients went on using charms such as this one for a sudden stitch –

> This to relieve the harm of the gods, this of elves,
> This to relieve the harm of the witch. I'll help you yet,
> So fly to the mountain top, you sprite!
> May the Lord help thee. Be you healed.

– but the scientific study of medicine never quite died out in England.

An age of contrasts

The Saxons show us the best and worst of human life existing side by side. Their savage cruelty and the hardships which they suffered in their efforts to win a living in a hostile land contrast with their search for law and justice and their achievements in art and learning. They helped to build a Christian civilization not only in England but in Europe also.

A seventh-century drinking horn from Taplow, Bucks.

Dates to remember

731 Bede finished his *History of the English Church and People*.
755 St Boniface was martyred in Germany.
800 Charles the Great was crowned Holy Roman Emperor on Christmas Day.

Things to do

1 Imagine that you are a Saxon accused of murder and write an account of your trial and punishment, if any.
2 Here is a diagram to show what was grown in three fields in each of three years. Copy the diagram, filling in the blanks.

	field 1	field 2	field 3
year 1	fallow		oats
year 2	barley	oats	
year 3	oats	fallow	

3 Find out all you can about Charles the Great, Alcuin, St Boniface and Bede.
4 The Saxons enjoyed riddles. Try to solve these. You will find pictures of the answers on pages 33 and 37.

(a) At times I am kissed so I speak
And call men to battle . . . At times I
Hang on a wall, all gleaming with gold
While men feast and drink . . .
Now say what I'm called.

(b) My nose bent to the ground, I dig in the earth
And rummage about, and move as he wills,
My grey old lord, fighting the forest . . .
What I bite with my teeth is pushed to one side,
If my lord and master handles me right.

5 Look at the plan of a Saxon town on page 38. Make a list of all the features which make it a good centre for trade.

Books to read

M. and C. H. B. Quennell, *Everyday Life in Roman and Anglo-Saxon Times*, Batsford
J. Finnemore, *Social Life in England*, Volume I, Black
E. Osmond, *Villages*, Batsford

Chapter 5
Alfred and the Vikings

The coming of the Vikings

'From the fury of the Northmen, Good Lord deliver us.' Many Saxons must have muttered this prayer as the growing peace of their land was shattered by the Vikings.

These men of Norway and Denmark found it hard to keep their families by fishing and farming the infertile slopes of the fiords. Instead they set out to rob the wealthy monasteries and villages of England. Their dragon ships glided smoothly along the coast or up river until they came to some unlucky settlement. The warriors leapt quickly ashore and began their work of killing, looting, and burning. They then made a quick getaway before the Saxons could raise an army to meet them in battle!

A Viking ship from Gokstadt, Norway, now in the Oslo Museum. It is over 70 feet long and the rudder is at the side, not the stern. In 1893, a copy was built and successfully sailed to the United States.

Viking life

The Vikings spent much of their time in sailing and fighting. As you can see from the photograph, Viking ships were built for speed rather than for comfort on a long journey. In spite of this, Norse adventurers sailed all round northern Europe and the Mediterranean. They may even have reached America long before Columbus. Russia is said to get its name from the Viking leader, Rurik the Red. He and his followers founded settlements there after long journeys by river and over land.

On such adventures the Vikings looked for the help and comfort of their gods. Like the pagan Saxons they worshipped Odin (Woden), king of the gods, and Thor the thunderer, God of War. They also had the belief that the souls of warriors who died fighting would be carried off by the Valkyries, war-like maidens, to the hall of Valhalla in Odin's palace. There the brave feasted and enjoyed themselves as they did on earth. In contrast, a man who died a 'cow's death' in bed could expect only the darkness of hell.

There was a lighter side to Viking life, however. The warriors returned home to a hall which looked similar to a Saxon hall. Dressed in their brightest cloaks and wearing magnificent gold

Two carvings from ninth-century Viking ships. *Above:* one found in the river Scheldt in the Netherlands; *below:* from the Oseberg ship in Norway. It belonged to a king and was the burial place of a princess. (Compare with the prows of the ships on page 53.)

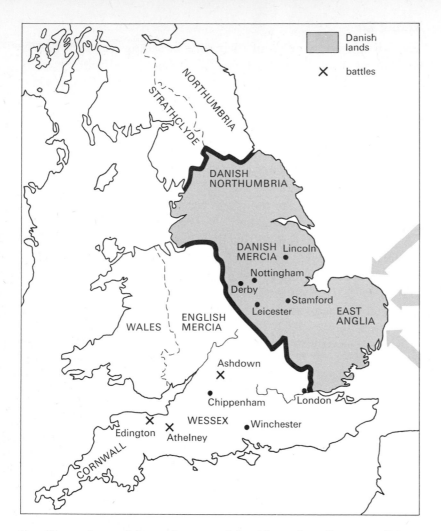

Danish lands

× battles

DANISH NORTHUMBRIA

NORTHUMBRIA

STRATHCLYDE

DANISH MERCIA

Lincoln
Nottingham
Derby
Stamford
Leicester

WALES

ENGLISH MERCIA

EAST ANGLIA

Ashdown
×

Chippenham

London

Edington
×

Athelney
×

WESSEX

Winchester

CORNWALL

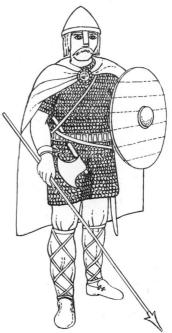

A Viking warrior.

jewellery, they celebrated successful raids and trading expeditions with their families who had been left behind to farm the land around the settlement. Everyone feasted and drank as tales were told of old battles and deeds of valour. No doubt many of the Viking women tried not to think of the time when their men must set out once more in search of treasure and adventure.

Resistance from Wessex

At first the Vikings showed no signs of wishing to settle down in England, but in 865 a huge army arrived. It was led by Ivar the Boneless and his brother Halfdan, one of the most famous of all Vikings. This time the Norsemen were prepared to stay. The Saxon kingdoms seemed too disunited to organize a proper defence. The kings of Wessex were powerful enough to claim the title of 'Bretwalda', which meant that other kings looked to their leadership. Yet even they could not make their subjects leave home to fight off the Vikings in some other part of the country. Still, it was Alfred, a king of Wessex, who came to lead English resistance to the invaders.

Alfred's early life

Alfred's childhood was happy and carefree, for he was a younger son and did not expect to become king. He learnt to hunt, to fight and to enjoy the poetry which told of the great deeds of the Saxon people. When he was only eleven, he went with his father on a visit to the Pope in Rome and so he knew much more of the outside world than most Saxons.

He first rode out to meet the Vikings in the company of his brother, King Ethelred. At Ashdown they faced an army which had already conquered Northumbria and East Anglia without much trouble and expected to do the same to Wessex. Both armies were divided into two, but Alfred and his men had to begin alone because his brother was still at prayer. He charged the enemy like a wild boar. At first the Vikings stood firm, but when Ethelred's troops arrived, they turned and ran. A poem written about a later battle shows us what the fighting must have been like:

> A roar filled the air. Warriors mightily hurled
> Deadly darts and the sharpest of spears.
> Busily bows twanged and shields were battered.
> Bitter was the battle and the slaughter
> On both sides. Young men lay lifeless.

Tomb-stone showing Vikings unfurling the sails of their ship.

A king on the run

Alfred became king on the death of his brother soon after the battle of Ashdown. The earlier years of his reign were full of defeat and retreat. Mercia fell to the Norsemen and so did all Wessex east of Selwood. Alfred and a few faithful warriors took refuge in the marshes round Athelney. His position seemed hopeless. It is to this part of his life that the legend of how he burned the cakes belongs.

Yet slowly the men of Wessex fought back. They used their knowledge of the countryside to make a series of surprise attacks on Danes who left camp. Finally, Alfred managed to gather together an army which met the invaders at Edington and defeated them so badly that the Danish leaders came to terms in their camp at Chippenham.

47

Alfred's triumph

King Guthrum and his leading men were all baptized as Christians with Alfred as chief godfather. They then left Wessex never to return. By 886 Alfred had won back part of Mercia from the Danes, including London, the natural capital of England. He then made a treaty with Guthrum which settled the boundary between the lands under Alfred's control and Danish lands (the Danelaw) which you can see marked on the map on page 46. After this all English people except those who were under the power of the Danes accepted Alfred as their leader.

Preparations were also made in case of future attack. A small fleet was built. Its ships were twice as big as those of the Vikings and carried thirty pairs of oars. No other king in Europe saw so clearly as Alfred that a strong navy is the best way of defeating raiders from the sea. Alfred also planned a series of forts to guard the countryside and tried to keep an army always at the ready. His big problem was that the men who fought in the fyrd, the Saxon army, kept running back home to look after their lands and families. Alfred divided the fyrd into two and sent half the men home for six months while the rest were kept ready to fight. Fewer men then deserted. In 892 another Danish army appeared, but the defences of Wessex held firm.

Peace restored

Alfred ruled as successfully in time of peace as he did in war. He believed his people's minds must be cared for as well as their bodies and tried to encourage the spread of religion and learning which had been stopped by the Danish invasions. Learned men were invited from other parts of England and Europe to begin schools and monasteries. One of them, Asser, wrote a life of Alfred, which is how we know so much about him. A school was begun in the palace at Winchester where children of rich and poor alike might come to learn. Craftsmen, such as builders and goldsmiths, were encouraged to work in Wessex and to teach their skills.

The king was not content to leave learning to others. He could not read English until he was twelve, but at thirty-eight he learned Latin so that he could translate some of the greatest Latin books into English for his people to read. Among these were a book by Pope Gregory who had sent Augustine to England, and Bede's history of the English Church. Alfred also brought out a new set of laws which protected the poor and encouraged men to be loyal to their lords.

The Alfred jewel. It bears the portrait of a king, probably Alfred himself, holding two sceptres. At the side are the words 'AELFRED ordered me to be made', worked in gold. The stem of the jewel is shaped into a boar's head.

A penny of Alfred's reign. Coins can give us a clue as to what the Saxon kings looked like, though the portraits on them are not true likenesses.

England's darling

Although often ill and in pain, Alfred was always kind, generous, and easy to approach. Yet this was not the only reason why he was known as 'England's darling'. He was the first Saxon king to rule not by fear but with the free consent and love of his people. Edward the Elder, Alfred's son, succeeded in winning back the Danelaw, so that he controlled all England up to the boundaries with Wales and Scotland. The coming of the Vikings and Alfred's resistance had changed the English from a group of warring tribes into one nation.

Dates to remember

793	The Vikings raided Lindisfarne
878	Alfred's victory at Edington
about 920	Edward the Elder became overlord of England, Scotland and Wales

Things to do

1   Imagine you are a Viking who fought at Ashdown and give your side of the story.
2   What do we mean by civilization? Do you think Alfred did much to save it in England?
3   Many places where the Danes settled have names that end in 'by' or 'thorp'. See how many of these you can find from a map of England. Why are most of them in the east Midlands and the north?

Alfred's translation of a book by Pope Gregory the Great, made between 890 and 897. This copy was made for Iverferth, Bishop of Worcester.

Books to read

C. A. Burland, *The Vikings*, Hulton Educational Publications.
Carola Oman, *Alfred, King of the English*, Dent.

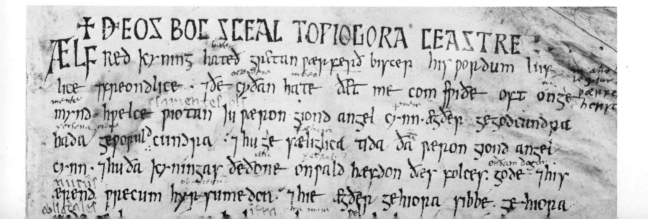

Chapter 6
Duke William and the Norman Conquest

England's weakness

For a time the English kings who came after Alfred and Edward continued their success against the Danes; but at last the crown passed to Ethelred the Redeless (ill-advised). He foolishly tried to buy the Danes off at one moment and to murder them the next. Finally the Danish King, Canute, turned him off the throne. Ethelred's son, Edward the Confessor, was called back from exile in Normandy to become king in 1042, but, as his name suggests, he was more interested in praying and confessing his sins than in ruling. He made little attempt to control the powerful nobles. One of these, Harold, the son of Earl Godwin, wanted the throne for himself.

Edward, however, had other plans. He saw that England had become cut off from the Continent during the time of Danish rule and was in danger of becoming part of Scandinavia. To stop this, Edward, who had no children of his own, decided that William of Normandy, his cousin by marriage, should be the next king of England.

William's strength

Few rulers have had so stormy a youth as William and lived to enjoy such success. He was born the son of a servant girl and the Duke of Normandy. When he was eight, his father died and William spent some time on the run from a half-brother who considered the boy to be a threat to his power. After years of hardship and danger he made himself Duke of Normandy, a land settled by the Norsemen over a century before. No man dared disobey him. He was strong enough to think of extending his power across the Channel to England.

Harold's claim to the throne

We can follow the story of the struggle between William and Harold from the Bayeux tapestry. This was embroidered in honour of the Norman victory and was most likely ordered by Bishop Odo of the town of Bayeux in Normandy, where it remains to this day. The first scene shows us the famous story of

how Harold swore to be faithful to William while on a visit to Normandy. Later it was said that he did not know he had his hand on a chest containing holy relics, the bones of saints, as he took the oath.

The next pictures show us the death of Edward the Confessor and Harold's coronation which followed. The crowd which is seen cheering the new king was probably not a large one. Although Harold had the advantage of being an Englishman and was elected by the Witan, he had no claim to the throne by birth and many of the other nobles were jealous of the Godwin family.

Scenes from the Bayeux Tapestry. *Above:* Harold swears an oath to William on chests concealing holy relics. *Below:* the funeral of Edward the Confessor. The king's body is carried to Westminster Abbey, which he had just built. God's hand can be seen, giving His blessing.

ERVNT:HAROLDO: NA: REGIS hIC RE REX:AN SIDET:HAROLD GLORVM: STIGANT ARCHIEPS

The landing near Hastings

The tapestry then shows us the building and launching of the Norman fleet, the landing at Pevensey and the Normans' first meal ashore. What is not shown is the attack made by Harold's brother, Tostig, and his ally, Harald Hardrada, the King of Norway, in the north of England just as William set sail. In reply to Hardrada's claim to the English kingdom, Harold granted him *'only seven feet of English earth for a grave, or perhaps a little more as he is a tall man'*. At Stamford Bridge the first invaders were defeated. Harold then rode south to deal with the Normans.

Above: Harold is offered the crown, and then appears seated on the throne while the sword of state is held on his right and the crowd outside applauds.
Below: meanwhile the Normans build William's fleet.

MAR E · TRAN · SIVIT

Above: The invasion fleet sets sail, taking with them the cavalry horses. *Below:* the first meal on English soil. Servants carry the food on spits to a makeshift table. Bishop Odo sits at the centre of the round table, saying grace. On his right sits William.

Within thirteen days he had returned to London and gathered more troops to make up for those foot-soldiers who had not been able to keep up with him. Unfortunately, he did not wait until all the English were assembled. He had more troops than William, but they were not well trained apart from the royal bodyguard, the house-carls. The English were not skilled in the use of archers in battle. Nor were they a match for the powerful Norman cavalry, for although they were good horsemen, they fought on foot. The Normans, however, were trained in the most up-to-date methods of warfare.

hIC·FECERVN:·PRANDIVM:· ET·hIC·EPISCOPVS·CIBV·ET·POTV:·BE NE DIC IT·

The battle

This scene from the tapestry shows how Harold had drawn up his men on a hill. It is probable that he was surprised by the sudden approach of the Normans who were well arranged with their archers in front, foot-soldiers in the next line and knights at the rear. The Saxons were all bunched together and began to defend their position grimly, knowing that no help would come.

Yet at first they seemed likely to win. The English battle-axes cut into the armour of the Norman knights, and some of the enemy turned tail and ran. At this point, Duke William appeared

Saxons defending a hill. Both sides suffered heavy casualties.

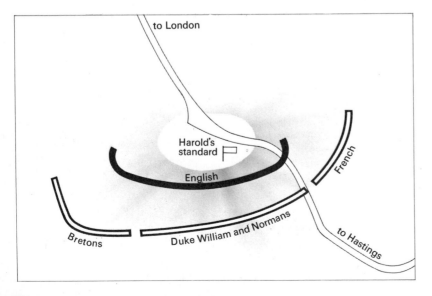

Battle lines at Hastings.

Above: A Saxon is hit in the eye by an arrow. The name 'Harold' is written above. *Below:* the death of Harold.

in their path. Rather than face the anger of their leader, they hurriedly set about attacking the English again.

They found that their flight had done what their fighting had failed to do. The English shield wall had crumbled. Harold had been unable to control his men, and they had broken ranks to chase the enemy down the hill. Soon all was confusion on the English side. Harold is said to have been killed by an arrow which pierced his eye. In the picture above you can see a man dying in this way. Look below and you will see that the words, 'HAROLD REX INTERFECTUS EST' which means 'Harold the

king was killed', are really over a man being cut down by a Norman horseman. Some people think this is how Harold really died. The house-carls fought on to avenge their lord until nearly all lay dead or wounded about the royal banner.

The Conquest

The battle of Hastings is one of the few battles which do really mark a turning point in a country's history. After it, William defeated English resistance in the west and the north, which he laid waste so that it did not recover for many years. In the marshes round Ely, Hereward the Wake continued the struggle for a time, even defying the Normans' secret weapon, a witch who shrieked curses from a high tower which the English eventually burnt. Yet there was no other real king for the English except William. The last surviving children of the royal house of Wessex fled to Scotland and made no attempt to return.

Slowly William brought the country under control. He built a network of castles from which his Norman followers could ride out to stop any trouble in the surrounding countryside. Then he ordered a survey of England called the Domesday Book, which would show him exactly what his new realm contained, and what

The two volumes of the Domesday Book, written in 1086, on top of an iron-bound chest in which they were kept at Westminster.

taxes its people could be expected to pay. It is said that not even a pig or a cow escaped the notice of William's men.

The new nobility

The manors or villages of England were shared out among Norman barons, abbots and bishops, who replaced English nobles. Each of these tenants-in-chief, as they were called, knelt before the king and clasped his hand. He then swore to be loyal to his royal master against all other men. This ceremony is known as doing homage. As well as this he had to provide a certain number of knights for the king in time of need.

The barons then settled knights on their lands. In return for being made lord of the manor, the knight took an oath of homage to his overlord and promised to fight for him when necessary, unless this would mean being disloyal to the king. Freemen and villeins held land from the lord of the manor where they lived, and repaid him by working on his land (the demesne), or serving in the manor house. A freeman could leave his lord's service and go away, though he rarely did so. In contrast, the villein had to stay on the manor where he was born.

The holding of land in return for service to a lord became known as the feudal system. It worked very well in King William's time because there was a shortage of gold and silver which could be used to pay rents in money. When the people of the manor wanted to buy something, they usually exchanged one lot of goods for another.

After the Conquest

So successful was William in tightening his grip on England, that at the time of his death the country had never been so peaceful. It was said that a man laden with gold could walk anywhere and no one would dare to rob him. With the king's encouragement, the Church also grew in strength. In the time of Archbishop Lanfranc new dioceses were formed and new monasteries founded. For the first time since the Romans left, England was in close contact with the mainland of Europe as William kept Normandy and other lands in France under his control and spent much of his time there. In future years some of the best leaders of the English Church and some of the most able servants of the English king came from France.

William was the sort of man who is feared rather than loved, but an Englishman who had been at his court and hated him for his grasping meanness was forced to admit:

The church at Iffley, Oxfordshire, built between 1175 and 1182. The wide rounded arches with geometric patterns are typically Norman. (Compare page 66.)

He was a man of great wisdom and strength of character, more powerful and honourable than all before him. Though he was as stern as possible to all those who defied him, he was kind to good men who loved God.

William would have asked no better epitaph.

Dates to remember

1066 The Norman Conquest of England
1085 Domesday Book was begun

Things to do

1 Study the illustrations taken from the Bayeux tapestry. Describe what you can find out from them about the weapons, methods of fighting, ships, clothes and cooking of the time.
2 Find the drawing of a castle on page 97. Why were these castles so difficult to capture and such a good way of controlling the countryside around?
3 Read this extract from the Domesday Book:

> William de Percy holds Hambledon. He came by it along with his wife. Alwin held it from King Edward. It was then taxed as 8 hides. There is land for 3 ploughs. There is 1 plough on the demesne. Also there are 6 villeins and 6 bordars (cottagers) with 2 ploughs. There are 2 serfs and a mill worth 12 pence. There is a woodland worth 4 swine. In Edward's reign it was worth 4 pounds as it is now. When it first came to its present lord it was worth 3 pounds.

TERRA WILLI DE PERCI. ~~IN MANESTOCHS~~.
Witts de pci ten AMBLEDUNE. cu femina sua accep.
Aluuin tenuit de rege. E. Tc 7 m se defd p una hida. Tra e
iii. car. In dnio. e una. 7 vi. uitti 7 vi. bord cu. ii. car.
Ibi. ii. serui. 7 molin de. xii. den. Silua de. iiij. porc
T.R.E. 7 m. uat. iiii. lib. Cu accep. iii. lib.

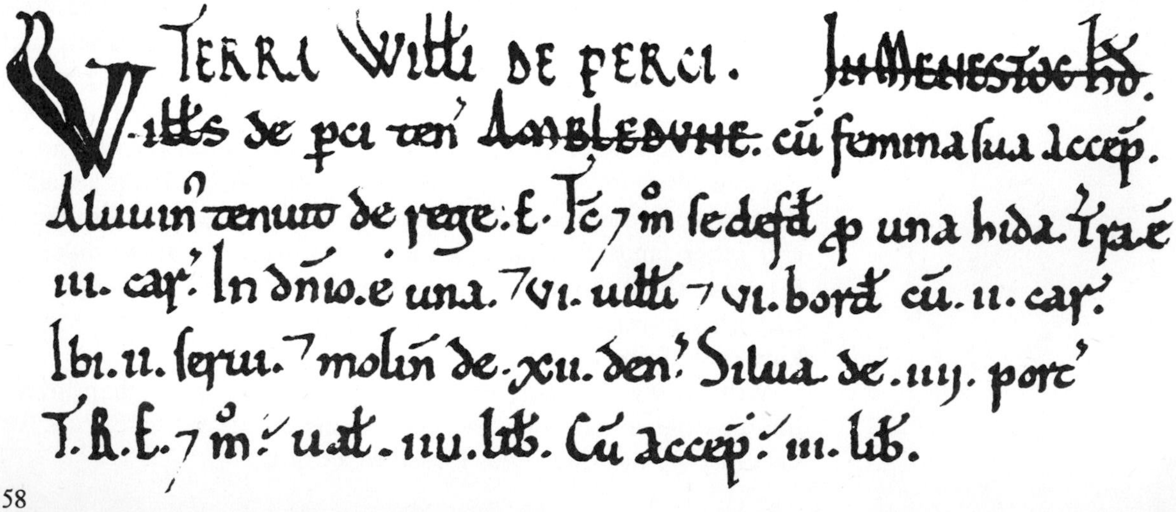

The entry about Hambledon in the Domesday Book. It was written in Latin with many of the words shortened to save time and space.

(a) How did de Percy come to hold Hambledon?

(b) Who held it before the Norman Conquest?

(c) How many people lived on the manor?

(d) What were the most valuable things on the manor?

(e) Did the manor become worth less at the time of the Norman Conquest, and if so, why?

Books to read

E. Luckock, *William the Conqueror*, Wheaton

R. A. Brown, *Castles*, Batsford

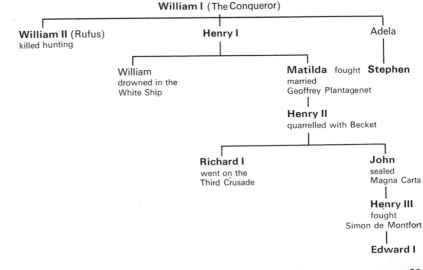

Norman and Plantagenet kings.

Chapter 7
Thomas Becket and the struggle between Church and State

Thomas Becket began life as the clever, worldly son of a Norman merchant who had settled in England. He ended it as a saint and was laid to rest in a magnificent tomb in Canterbury Cathedral. The question which has puzzled people ever since is whether he was really a holy man or just a humbug.

The king's problem

King Henry II was in no doubt about the answer. He believed that Becket was a traitor who had betrayed him instead of helping him to solve his most difficult problems. As you can see from the chart on page 59, Henry, the first Plantagenet king, came to the throne at the end of a civil war between his mother, Matilda, and her cousin, Stephen. He found that the barons had been acting as they pleased while there was no strong king to check them. His first problem was to keep them in order, therefore.

Henry's second problem was how to tighten his hold over the churchmen whose lands provided him with money and knights to fight in his wars. Like other Norman kings, he wanted to choose his own bishops and to make rules for the other clergy. Yet he knew this would not be easy. Already on the Continent Pope Gregory VII had quarrelled with the Emperor Henry IV and tried to free the Church in Germany and Italy from his control. In England Henry's great-uncle, William Rufus, had been on very bad terms with his archbishop, Anselm, as you have read on page 10. So Henry was prepared for trouble from the clergy. He looked for a way of making it as little as possible.

Becket's early career

The king believed that Becket could help him to solve both his problems. He knew that the clever young man had been to a grammar school and that his main interest was the law. Although he was a clergyman, Becket spent most of his time in helping Henry to deal with the barons. Part of his work in the office of chancellor was to force them to destroy castles which they had built without permission and to stop them from trying cases which should have come before the king's judges.

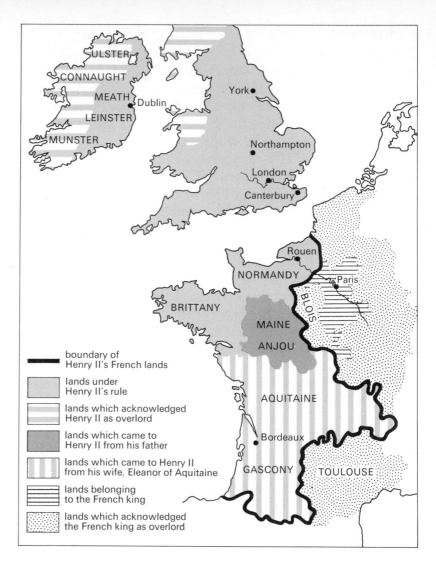

ULSTER

CONNAUGHT

MEATH • Dublin

LEINSTER

MUNSTER

York •

Northampton •

London •

Canterbury •

Rouen •

NORMANDY

• Paris

BRITTANY

BLOIS

MAINE

ANJOU

AQUITAINE

• Bordeaux

GASCONY

TOULOUSE

▬▬ boundary of
Henry II's French lands

lands under
Henry II's rule

lands which acknowledged
Henry II as overlord

lands which came to
Henry II from his father

lands which came to Henry II
from his wife, Eleanor of Aquitaine

lands belonging
to the French king

lands which acknowledged
the French king as overlord

Left: Henry II's tomb. He was buried in 1189 at the Abbey of Fontevraud in France. Henry lived more in France than in England, and spoke more French than English.

Right: Henry II's empire.

Becket was rewarded by the king for his services with important posts in the Church, but he showed little love for the religious life. He never bothered to learn enough Latin to dare to preach when leading scholars were present. Once or twice he was told off by the Archbishop of Canterbury for not doing his duty to the Church. He always sided with the king when he wished to tax the clergy, and seemed to be the perfect royal servant. Becket was often to be seen at court wearing fashionable clothes and amusing himself in feasting, hunting or merely talking to the king. Henry had the bright idea of making Becket his next archbishop. Then the clergy would be led by a man who would not complain whatever he did to the Church.

A surprise for the king

Even before he agreed to become archbishop, Becket warned the king that he might change. Henry laughed off the suggestion and insisted that nothing would ever break their friendship. He soon found out his mistake. Instead of the finest silk next to his skin the new archbishop wore a rough hair shirt. His guests were still treated to fine food, but he dined on bread and water. He even had himself beaten as a sign of sorrow for past sins. The other bishops, who had been prepared to look down on Becket for his gay living, now grew jealous of his holiness and hated him all the more. The result was that when trouble came, the archbishop stood alone.

The quarrel

The Church had its own courts in which it tried all clergymen who were accused of a crime. Often they were given little or no punishment. For example, a priest called Philip of Brois murdered a knight, but was found 'not guilty' in the Church court. He refused to appear before the king's judges and, when Henry complained, Becket only had the murderer flogged. The king then demanded that once clergy had been found guilty in their own courts, they should be handed over to the royal courts for punishment. He claimed that this was the usual custom in England. The clergy, led by their archbishop, disagreed.

Pope Alexander was horrified by Becket's behaviour, for he wanted Henry's help against the Emperor of Germany who had driven him into exile. The archbishop then ruined his own case by giving in to the king's demands. As one of the bishops put it, 'It was our leader who turned his back, the captain of our camp who fled.' The king at once put a series of rules for the clergy into writing. Becket did not openly oppose him, although he still felt that priests should not be tried twice for the same crime.

The archbishop's flight

Soon, however, Becket changed his mind. He tried to leave the country, but failed. Henry called a meeting at Northampton and Becket was so sick with nerves that he could not go. The king cleverly tried to ruin him, not over the matter of the Church courts but over some money which he claimed Becket still owed him from the time when he was chancellor. At last the archbishop appeared, carrying a cross before him and certain that he was about to die. He was allowed to leave, however, with shouts of 'Traitor!' still ringing in his ears. Becket spent the next five years

Becket sailing into exile.

Becket and the king in argument. Behind the archbishop stand the four knights.

in exile abroad until, to everyone's surprise, he met Henry in Normandy and the quarrel was patched up.

The murder

The archbishop returned to England, but it soon became clear that nothing was changed. On Christmas day, 1170, he openly defied the king by excommunicating the bishops who had sided against him and some of the leading barons who had gone out of their way to annoy him by hunting on his lands without permission.

Henry had the quick temper of all the Plantagenet family. Sometimes he would roll on the floor, tearing his hair and biting his nails in fury. On this occasion he cried out 'O who will rid me of this nuisance of a priest!' At once, four of his knights set out before he could change his mind. Reginald Fitz Urse, William de Tracy, Hugh de Morville, and Richard le Breton travelled from the court in Normandy and reached Canterbury on 29 December.

On hearing of their coming, the monks dragged Becket into

the Cathedral in the hope that he would be safe in so holy a place. The archbishop refused to let them bar the door, however, and the knights rushed in crying 'Where is Thomas Becket, traitor to his king and country?' He calmly answered 'Here I am. I am no traitor, but a priest.' Becket then bowed his head in prayer. Fearing that the people might come to help the archbishop, Fitz Urse suddenly leapt on him and wounded him on the head. An eye-witness wrote later:

By the same blow he wounded the one who tells you this tale, for when other monks and priests fled, he kept close to the archbishop and cradled him in his arms until the one which he used to shield him was almost cut off. The saint received a second blow, but still stood. At the third blow he fell on all fours . . . and the third knight shattered his sword on the paving stones as he gave him a dreadful wound. The

Murder of St Thomas. As he falls, the priest (*right*) is slashed on the arm. The act made a deep impression and was painted repeatedly by medieval artists. This miniature of about 1200 may have been the first.

fourth knight kept guard for the others. The fifth man, who was a clerk, not a knight . . . put his foot on the holy martyr's neck and scattered his brains and blood over the floor, shouting to the others 'Let's be on our way, knights. He'll never rise again.'

Becket's victory

By his death, Becket triumphed over the king who had outwitted him in life. Henry found himself so unpopular that he gave up his attempt to pass sentence on the clergy in his own courts. He even allowed himself to be whipped through the streets of Canterbury by monks as a sign of his sorrow at the archbishop's death. Becket was proclaimed a saint and his fine tomb in Canterbury Cathedral was later visited by thousands of pilgrims. Although the kings of England still kept some control over the Church, none of them managed to defy the Pope with any success until the time of the Reformation in the sixteenth century.

The great age of the medieval Church

The power of the Church was also increasing on the Continent. The emperors of Germany were being weakened by troubles at home and were no longer such a threat to the various popes with whom they quarrelled. The Church was also reformed from within. St Bernard drew up a new and stricter rule of life for his monks at Clairvaux and Cîteaux. The Cistercians, as his followers were called, went out to found monasteries in all parts of Europe, especially in wild and lonely places where they tilled the soil or took to sheep-farming. The ruins of their great houses are still to be seen at Melrose, Rievaulx, and Tintern in Britain today. In addition the Pope could count on the support of two new orders of friars who were directly under his command.

One of these was founded by Francis of Assisi who began life as the gay, pleasure-loving son of a wealthy merchant. During a serious illness his thoughts turned to God and his whole life changed. To the horror of his father, who tried to lock him up as a madman, he gave up his worldly goods and went round in rags, preaching and looking after the sick, especially the lepers whom no one else would touch. He got what money he needed by begging or working. His followers also lived like this at first, although later they built their own houses, usually in the poorest part of a town, and tended to wander around less. Like their leader, the early Franciscan friars were famous not only for their kindness and holiness, but for the joy which they found in God and his creation.

Badges of St Thomas were sold at Canterbury, and pilgrims visiting his tomb would buy and wear them, perhaps on their hats.

65

The Norman style 1066–1150.
The nave of Durham Cathedral
shows the round-headed
Norman arches. The diagrams
below show the structures of
the naves and windows.

The Early English style
1150–1250. The old choir of
Canterbury Cathedral which Becket
knew was destroyed by fire and had
to be rebuilt. Arches became
more pointed, and roofs higher.

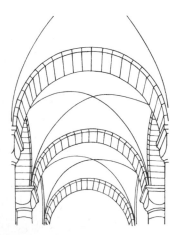

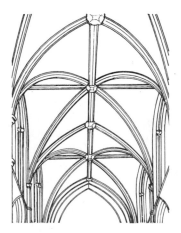

The Decorated style 1250–1350. The choir of Exeter Cathedral shows the great variety of carved decorations. As building methods improved, it became possible to make much larger windows, and glass-making became a work of art.

The Perpendicular style 1350–1550. Windows became even larger and, here at Gloucester Cathedral, filled a whole wall. Arches were less pointed and met in star-shaped patterns at the vault.

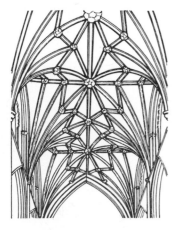

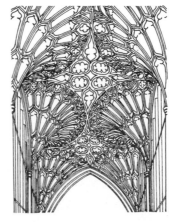

The other order of friars was founded by the Spaniard, St Dominic. He saw how easily false beliefs could spread, especially in the growing towns. He and his followers, the Dominicans, set out to preach the Christian faith and explain it to the people. Some of them arrived in England in 1221, three years before the first Franciscans. Unlike the monks, both types of friar spent their time in the world, preaching and looking after the needy.

Thanks to the efforts of the great men who served it, the medieval Church was able to keep its independence and cure its own weaknesses. The spires and towers of medieval churches which still dot the British countryside are silent witnesses to its age of glory.

The habits of some of the religious orders, from left to right: Cistercians in white, Dominicans in black over white, Premonstatensians in white, Austin friars, Franciscans, Carmelites and Benedictines.

A friar preaching from a pulpit.

Dates to remember

1112   Bernard became a monk at Cîteaux
1170   Becket was murdered
1224   The first Franciscans arrived in England

Things to do

1   Find out what you can about Lanfranc, Gregory VII, Anselm, St Bernard and St Dominic.
2   Imagine you are the monk who was with Becket at his death. Explain what happened and why you defended him.
3   Here is a message to the monks of Winchester from Henry II:

I order you to hold free election, but I forbid you to elect anyone except Richard my clerk, the Archdeacon of Poitiers.

Why do you think that Henry chose Richard to be the new bishop? Do you think the Pope would have approved?
4   The power and wealth of the Church was often shown in its buildings. Study the drawings of church architecture on pages 66–7. Try to find out where there are other buildings in each of the styles shown.
5   Here is part of a poem written by St Francis. How does it fit in with what you know of his life and work?

Praise be to Thee, Lord, for all Thy creatures,
Above all Brother Sun
Who brings us the day and lends us his light . . .
Praise be to Thee, Lord, for Sister Earth
Who feeds and keeps us, and bears
Fruit of all kinds, with colourful flowers and plants.
Praise be to Thee, Lord, for those who pardon each other
In love of Thee, and have to bear
Sickness and suffering . . .
Blessed are those who do Thy will,
For death cannot harm them.

Books to read

I. Doncaster, *The Medieval Church*, Longmans
E. Vale, *Cathedrals*, Batsford

Chapter 8
Richard the Lion-heart and the Third Crusade

A divided family

In 1189 the great King Henry II lay dying almost alone. A few miles away, his eldest son, Richard, knelt in homage to King Philip of France, his father's chief enemy. The two had just forced the old man to make a humiliating peace. In the palace at Winchester Henry is said to have kept the picture of an eagle being pecked to death by its four young eaglets. He explained that they were:

My four sons who do not stop persecuting me even unto death. The youngest of them whom I now love so much will do me more harm than the others in the end.

Henry's opinion was quite right because John was not only the cause of the revolt against him (Richard was jealous of the lands his young brother had been given), but also became one of its leaders. When news of his death reached Henry's grim wife, Eleanor of Aquitaine, she must have felt a glow of triumph. She had her revenge on the husband who had imprisoned her. Her plan of turning his own sons against him had at last succeeded.

Richard and John

Richard's first deeds as king show him at his best and worst. He rewarded the men loyal to his father because he admired those who stood by their friends and acted honestly. He then went on to make the same mistake as his father and gave his worthless young brother John six counties to rule as a small present. He became almost a king within his brother's kingdom. To make matters worse, Richard, who was a superb soldier, decided to go on a crusade. He spent four months in England and placed it in the care of William Longchamp, an able but unpleasant man. Prince John found it easy to plot his fall from power. Meanwhile Richard set out for the Holy Land. No one thought he would return.

How the crusades began

The First Crusade had set out in 1095, after pilgrims had returned

A knight kneeling in homage to his overlord, the king. Richard I took such an oath to the French king for his lands on the Continent.

from visiting the holy places where Jesus lived and told tales of the cruel treatment they had received at the hands of the Turks who had conquered Palestine. These Turks were Muslims, followers of the prophet Mohammed. He was born at Mecca in Arabia about A.D. 570, and came to believe that there was only one God (Allah) and that Jesus was not the son of God but only a prophet. Mohammed promised rewards in heaven for those who fought for their faith. After his death his followers conquered much of the Middle East, North Africa and Spain. There the Muslims quickly became interested in the learning of Greece and Rome so that they were often more civilized than the Christians of Western Europe. Once they had a country in their power, they were often tolerant to people of another religion and allowed them to worship freely. The Turks' ill-treatment of the pilgrims to the Holy Land was unusual.

There were many reasons why the plan to send a crusading army against the Muslim Turks was popular. The Church approved because by encouraging and helping to organize the expedition, the Pope, Urban II, showed himself to be one of the most powerful men in Europe. Kings and princes joined in because as the population of Western Europe grew, there was a land shortage. They hoped to win territory in Palestine where landless men might settle. Also they might find it easier to keep the peace if their more lively and rebellious subjects could be shipped away to cause trouble to the Turks instead of at home. At the same time, European trade was recovering from the effects of the barbarian invasions which had nearly destroyed it. Merchants saw the chance of trading in the silks and spices of the East. When the crusades began, however, the chief reason

Tomb of a crusader at the Temple church of St Mary, Farringdon, London.

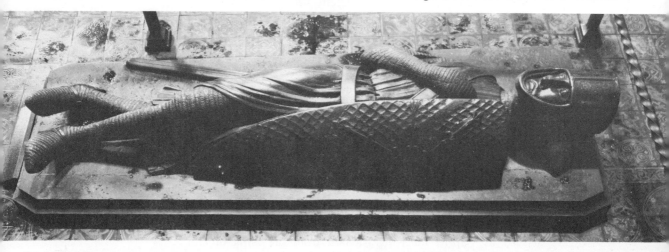

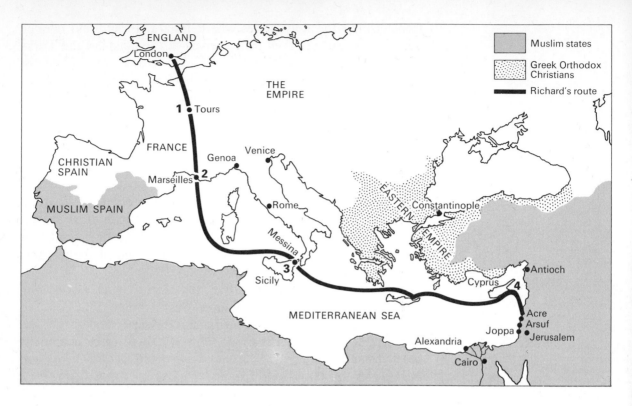

for going was love of Christ, hatred of the Infidel who occupied the places where he had lived, and the wish to make up for past sins by fighting to regain the Holy Land.

The Third Crusade   1189–92

The news that the work of earlier expeditions had been largely undone and that Saladin had retaken Jerusalem, caused Richard and the other crusaders to set out. You can trace his journey on the map which also shows you something of what happened to the king on his travels. We are lucky to have an account of the crusade written by someone who served Richard and saw most of the events he describes. Here is part of his story:

What Richard was like

Richard was tall and handsome with reddish-brown hair. His limbs were supple and straight and no one was better at drawing a sword quickly and using it well. His good character and habits added to the powerful and dignified impression made by his graceful appearance.

Richard's arrival at Acre

Messengers arrived at Cyprus for King Richard from the King of

Europe at the time of the Third Crusade.
1 Richard received the scrip and staff of a pilgrim.
2 He embarked for the Holy Land.
3 He quarrelled with the Sicilians and stormed Messina.
4 Richard captured Cyprus from the Greeks and married Princess Berengaria of Navarre.

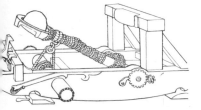

Above: besieging a town. The defenders try to ward off the enemy with stones and arrows, and swing a large stone on the end of a rope. The besiegers bring up a heavy battering ram, and are digging to undermine the walls, under protection of covered vehicles. Others struggle with a kind of crane *(left)* to lift soldiers on to the battlements. *Below:* a ballista for throwing giant stones at the enemy.

France. They begged him to come quickly to the siege of Acre because no attack could be made without him. Because he refused to hurry they slandered him by saying he was wasting his time in useless activity when innocent Christians were being tormented by the Saracens (Turks). . . . All the people rejoiced greatly at Richard's long-awaited arrival and the meeting of the French and English. Their two kings stood aside to let each other pass through the gate, and treated each other with every show of courtesy. Then Richard withdrew to his tent to plan the campaign.

The siege of Acre

In the siege he used ballistae for throwing stones and many darts and javelins. Also, his men dug tunnels underneath the towers from which the Saracens were firing. They undermined the foundations and made a blaze with wood so that the stone cracked and the towers fell down. Day and night the Christians attacked the walls. The Turks were so full of wonder and fear that some threw themselves off the walls by night and others begged to be baptized. . . . Saladin, thinking it would be dangerous to delay, came to terms.

Richard's quarrel with the King of France

In the course of time the two kings had a fierce quarrel (over the sharing out of land). The King of France said he had caught a disease as an excuse for giving up his crusading vows; but really he was as fit as when he first took the cross.

The fate of Richard's prisoners

After Richard decided on the advice of his men not to wait any longer for the hard-hearted Saladin to ransom the Turkish prisoners, they were all beheaded except for a few of the nobles who might be exchanged for Christian captives.

The battle of Arsuf

Richard the King saw the army thrown into confusion as they met the Turks, but he spurred his horse on . . . into a crowd of Turkish soldiers. They fell back from him to right and left. Many were seen there after the battle: some bewailing their fate, some dying as they lay in their own blood. Many mangled bodies were heedlessly trampled underfoot.

Retreat from Jerusalem

After twice seeing the walls of Jerusalem in the distance, the crusaders could not agree on their next move and turned back. Richard then held talks with Saladin and seems to have found him more likeable and trustworthy than some of his fellow-

Richard I tearing the cross from Saladin (right). The dead are trampled underfoot.

Christians. The two warriors paid generous compliments to each other and when the English king had a fever, Saladin kindly sent him a gift of peaches, pears, and snow from a nearby mountain to cool his drinks. Richard even offered to let Safadin, Saladin's brother, marry his sister Joan.

Permission was granted for Christian pilgrims to visit Jerusalem, but apart from this the Third Crusade had few obvious results. Its real importance was that it increased trade between the eastern Mediterranean and Europe in such precious goods as muslin (cotton), damask (silk, named after Damascus), spices, oils, perfumes, and fruits such as plums, melons, dates and figs. Richard, however, was not interested in this nor in the knowledge of mathematics, medicine and astronomy which the Christians also got from the Turks. To him the crusade was a failure because he had to leave the holy places in the hands of the Infidel.

Richard's return

Sadly, Richard sailed for home. Already he had learnt of the treacherous friendship of his brother John and Philip of France, who was eager to conquer the English lands in his kingdom. On the way home Richard was captured by the Duke of Austria

A castle built by the crusaders in Syria during the twelfth century. It fell to the Saracens after a heavy siege in 1271.

whom he had offended by tearing up an Austrian flag planted in the city of Acre. Still most of his lands remained loyal and collected the huge ransom demanded for his release. The French king sent a message to John: 'Look to yourself, the devil is loosed.'

It needed only two months of Richard's time to set England in order. He then went off again to fight King Philip from his headquarters at Chateau Gaillard.

On 6 April 1199, he died after being struck in the shoulder by an arrow while trying to punish a baron who had quarrelled with him over some treasure.

Richard had grown fat and was no longer the handsome young king who had set out on crusade. Out of his ten years' reign he had been in England only six months. At times he showed himself to be as vain and cruel as the rest of his family. Yet he had a greatness of spirit and a genius for fighting which kept his people loyal in spite of all his brother John could do. His heart remained in the Holy Land, however, and it is best to remember the only English king who ever took part himself in a crusade with the words he spoke as he gazed at the coast of Palestine for the last time:

O Holy Land, I commend you to God and hope that by His Grace I may be granted enough time in which to save you.

A page of the Koran, the holy book of the Muslims. This copy was written in Egypt in 1304. Muslims were forbidden to draw the human form, so manuscripts were decorated with elaborate patterns, based on leaves and flowers.

Dates to remember

632   Mohammed died
1095   The crusades began
1189   Richard I set out on crusade
1291   The Turks recaptured the whole of Palestine

Things to do

1   Read the description of what Richard was like carefully, remembering that it was written by one of his friends. Then make a list of Richard's good and bad points from what you have read in the chapter. How far does his friend tell us the truth about him?
2   What can you learn about Richard's fighting methods from the story of his triumphs at Acre and Arsuf?
3   Find out all you can about the Muslim religion. Perhaps you will be able to find and read part of the Koran, its holy book.

4   After the crusades people in Europe began to use Arabic numerals, e.g., 1, 2, 3, 4, as we do today. Try to do a multiplication sum using the Roman numerals which were used before. Can you see why the Arabic numbers are so much better?
5   Many stories and films are set in the reign of King Richard. Try to remember as many of them as you can. What sort of man is King John in them?

Books to read

J. Williams, *Knights of the Crusades*, Cassell (A Caravel Book)
Alfred Duggan, *The Story of the Crusades*, Faber

Tomb of Richard I. He died in France and was buried beside his father at Fontevraud Abbey.

Chapter 9
An English traveller in the Middle Ages

Difficulties and dangers

One result of the crusades was that people became more interested in foreign travel. This was still very difficult. You can see from the fourteenth-century map of the world that little was known of geography. Try comparing it with a modern map. Travellers on land had the choice of riding on horse or mule or walking, perhaps with their baggage carried on a pack-mule. In Britain and the other countries of Europe there had been few new roads and bridges since Roman times, though sometimes a rich man might give money for them to be built as an act of charity. Often roads became pitted with ruts and holes. In winter they were so muddy that travel became impossible. Robbers lurked near the highways and it was never wise to journey alone or unarmed.

As you can see from the picture, ships were clumsy and top-heavy. In rough weather they tended to capsize, and on calm days they found it difficult to catch the wind. Many captains still plotted their course by the sun and stars, though compasses were made and used during the thirteenth century. Usually ships kept as near the coast as possible. It is not surprising that travellers preferred to go by land rather than by sea when they could.

Right: a map of the world, drawn in England in the late fourteenth century. Jerusalem is in the centre and England (Anglia) with all its castles in the bottom left-hand corner. In the bottom centre, the Pillars of Hercules mark the Straits of Gibraltar.

A carrack of the late fifteenth century. Although a merchant vessel, it was fitted for war: there are three cannons *(right),* and raised platforms for firing catapults.

Sir John de Mandeville

In spite of the slowness and dangers of travel, some brave explorers did venture abroad. One of the most popular books of the Middle Ages was written by a knight of St Albans called Sir John de Mandeville. He claimed to have spent thirty years touring such places as Palestine, Persia, Egypt, India and China. There are so many obvious mistakes in his book that some people think that he had not been to most of the places he describes, or even that Sir John never existed and that the whole book is made up of tales from a number of travellers. See what you think as you read some of them.

The world

And men may prove by reason and experience that it is possible to go by ship all round the world. Now you shall know that opposite the polar star is the other star called the antarctic. . . . These two stars are fixed; and about them all the heavens turn, as a wheel turns on its axle. It seems to simple and unlearned men that people may not go to the other side of the earth because they would fall off, but this may not be. Although it is possible to go round the world, only one in a thousand could return from such a journey, because there are a thousand ways to go and no one could be sure of finding his way home except by luck or the Grace of God. For the earth is very large – 20,425 miles in circumference as the old astronomers used to say; 31,500 as I believe.

India

In India there are many different kingdoms; it is called India from a river called Indus which runs through the country. In that river they find eels thirty feet long or more. The people who live near the country

John de Mandeville at work on one of the great travel books of this period.

A giraffe, drawn by the illustrator of Mandeville's book, according to the description.

80

are a nasty colour, green and yellow. Around India are five thousand inhabited islands. . . . In that country are snakes and vermin because of the great heat of the country and of the pepper. And when any man dies they burn his body and his wife with him if she has no child. . . . The Emperor, Prester John, is a Christian and a great part of his country also.

Islands of the East

In one of these islands are giants, hideous to look on, and they have only one eye in the middle of the forehead; they eat nothing but raw flesh and fish. In another isle to the South live a small, evil tribe who have no heads and their eyes are in their shoulders. . . . In another isle there are people with lips so big that they can cover their faces with them as they sleep in the sun. In another isle there are people with ears which hang down to their knees.

Cathay (China)

In this city called Caydon is the palace of the great Chan, which is the greatest and fairest in the world with a wall two miles long round it. And all about the palace are many different trees and great fishponds with many fair bridges. Within the palace in the hall are twenty-four golden pillars covered in red skins of panthers. . . . And at the head of the hall is the Emperor's throne where he sits to eat. It is of precious stone, bordered all about with gold, pearl and other jewels. The Emperor has a table to himself which is of crystal, gold and precious stones. And below this table sit four clerks who write down everything the Chan says, be it good or evil. At great feasts men bring birds made of gold to the Emperor's table and make them dance and sing and clap their wings. It is a pleasing sight though I do not know whether they do it by craft or by witch-craft. They are more skilled in the sciences than any other men in the world. . . . The people of the country wear long clothes without furs, made of silk and gold, split up the side and fastened with silk laces. The women wear the same as the men, and you can only tell the difference by the sign of a man's foot which women have on their foreheads to show that they are under a man's foot.

Each has a separate house which is round and made of wood, with one window above which lets in light and allows smoke to escape. . . . They eat all kinds of beasts except pigs, but they have only a little bread and no peas, nor beans, nor any soup except that which is made from meat. . . . And when they have eaten, they wipe their hands upon their skirts, for they have no napkins or towels except the great lords. And after a meal they put the unwashed dishes into the pot with the left-overs until they come to eat again. They live miserably and eat once a day only. In our country we eat twice as much. . . . Every man has a bow and arrows and a great axe. All the Tartars have small eyes and little hair except for a small beard.

Travellers' tales.

Marco Polo set out from Venice to explore the East before Mandeville's time. Here we see him with his father and his uncle at the Persian port of Ormuz where merchants from West and East met. 'Merchants come here by ship from India' wrote Marco Polo. The elephant in his boat is an Indian one.

Marco Polo examining peppers in Malabar, India. There was a ready market for the spices of the East in Europe.

Paper money in China. Marco Polo was surprised to see that when the Great Khan *(left)* and his officials had stamped their seals on the notes, they could be used as currency.

The Muslims

I will tell you of the laws and beliefs of the Saracen, which are found in the book called Alkoran. They say that among the prophets Jesus was the best and that he made the Gospels which are full of charity and truth to those that believe in God. They fast a month of the year, eating only at night. If anyone asks them what they believe, they say 'We believe in God, Creator of heaven and earth and all other things that were made. And without him nothing can be made. And we believe in the Day of Judgement, and that every man shall get what reward he has earned. And we hold all true that God has said through his prophets.' Also Mohammed commanded that they should have two, three, or four wives. This Mohammed reigned in Arabia in the year of Our Lord 610.

Dates to remember

1214   Genghis Khan began the Mongol dynasty which later ruled China and India

1271   Marco Polo set out on his travels to China

1322   Sir John de Mandeville claims he began his journey

Things to do

1   Find out about the shape and movement of the world and its place in the universe. Then compare it with Mandeville's ideas. Who was nearer to being right about the circumference of the earth – Mandeville or the old astronomers?

2   Try to find at least two points on which Mandeville was right about India and two points on which he was wrong.

3   Look at the drawings of natives on page 81. How do they fit Mandeville's strange description of them?

4   Make a list of the ways the Chinese were (a) ahead of (b) behind the people of England in Mandeville's day.

5   How does Mandeville's account of the Muslims agree with what you found out about them in the last chapter?

Books to read

R. J. Unstead, *Travel by Road through the Ages*, Black

R. J. Hoare, *Travel by Sea*, Black

M. Collis, *Marco Polo*, Faber

Chapter 10
Edward I and the beginning of a united Britain

Until the reign of Edward I the British Isles were far from being a united kingdom. Ireland, Wales and Scotland were ruled by native kings and princes, except for a few areas which had been conquered by English barons. Even in England itself there were divisions between the French-speaking barons and their English-speaking freemen and villeins, and between the barons and the king with whom they were often at war.

King against barons: the Magna Carta

Richard I's absence in the Holy Land and the expense of the crusade weakened the power of the Crown in England. When his brother John became king, he lacked the money to defend the English lands in France successfully. The meanness and cruelty of his character added to his unpopularity and the barons, supported by the Church and the leading citizens of London, rebelled against him.

John was forced to make peace with his enemies on the island of Runnymede in the Thames in 1215. In the Great Charter or Magna Carta, which he sealed there, he promised to keep the Church free and unharmed. He also tried to please the townsmen by granting safe conduct to any foreign merchant visiting England. The most important points which the king agreed to were:

Part of the Magna Carta, dated 15 June 1215. Only four copies still exist: two are in the British Museum, and two in the Cathedrals of Lincoln and Salisbury.

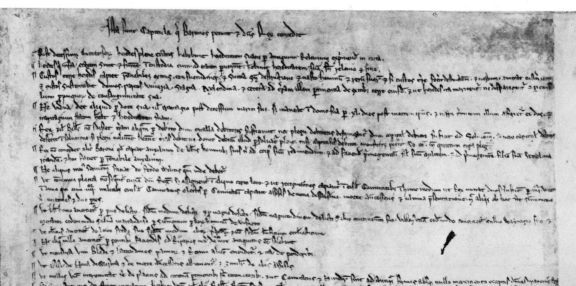

No scutage or aid (taxes) shall be demanded in our realm without the consent of the great council. . . . No freeman shall be arrested, put in prison, or lose his property, or be outlawed or banished, or harmed in any way . . . unless he has been judged by his equals under the law of the land. Justice will not be sold to anyone, nor will it be refused or delayed.

In later times Magna Carta has been used to prove that in England the subject has certain rights against the government which cannot touch him or his property unless the law allows it. You will notice, however, that in King John's time these rights only belonged to those of the rank of freeman or above. The villeins and serfs who far outnumbered them were not so fortunate.

Simon de Montfort

King John soon showed that he had no intention of keeping the promises which he had made. He died as the barons were once more rebelling against him. His heir was his young son, Henry III. During his long reign the barons continued their struggle to make the king obey the terms of the Great Charter. They were led by Simon de Montfort, the Earl of Leicester.

Earl Simon was a strange mixture of nobility and selfishness. He had married Eleanor, the king's sister, and it seemed likely that he would be Henry's friend. Unfortunately, the two men quarrelled. The king refused to pay the sum of money he had promised to the earl on her marriage. Then Simon told him that he should be locked up like the idiot king of France, Charles the Simple, for his folly in losing English lands in the south of France. Henry never forgave the insult.

The earl tried to make him rule with the advice of the barons' council. War broke out and Henry was defeated at Lewes. De Montfort then called a parliament, a meeting of barons, knights and townspeople, to help him restore peace and order. His triumph did not last long, however. The young Prince Edward came to his father's rescue and Earl Simon was killed at Evesham in 1265.

Edward's peace

When he became king on his father's death, Edward found it easy to keep his barons in order, for he had most of the qualities needed by the successful ruler in the Middle Ages. He was tall, silver-haired and dignified. Only a drooping eye-lid spoiled his handsome appearance. He had courage, determination, and a cool judgement in time of danger. He really tried to live up to his

The seal of Simon de Montfort, 1258. Seals were used instead of signatures on official documents.

motto of 'I keep my promises'. Most important, Edward had the intelligence to see that the barons would remain loyal, if it was in their interest to do so.

He therefore agreed to stand by the terms of the Great Charter. His laws were often as helpful to the barons as to himself. It is true that he ordered an inquiry into the rights of barons to hold their courts. Some could not prove their right and were no longer allowed to act as judges. Yet Edward was wise enough to take no action in such a case as that of William de Warenne, who drew his old rusty sword as the proof that he based his rights on his ancestors who had fought with the Conqueror in 1066.

Edward I's seal, showing him enthroned with orb and sceptre, 1276.

The growth of parliament

Like Simon de Montfort before him, the king came to believe that England was like a body in which all the parts must be made to work together. To help them to agree it was useful to have meetings of the council at which complaints could be heard, laws passed, and taxes approved. These meetings came to be called parliaments from the French word 'parler', to talk.

Edward copied Earl Simon in inviting not only the leading barons, but also two knights from each shire, and two leading citizens from each town, to his parliaments. In this way he was able to persuade the wealthy merchant class, who were profiting from increasing sales of English wool to Flanders, to pay higher taxes. Later, parliament became so big that it was easier for the barons and bishops to meet in one part of the Palace of Westminster and the knights and townsmen in another. So began the House of Lords and the House of Commons.

The English in Ireland

Edward was forced to demand such large taxes from his parliaments because he wished to make the rest of the British Isles into one kingdom under his control, just as England was. Only in Ireland did he try to do this without the use of force. The country had been conquered by the English barons led by Richard Strongbow, Earl of Pembroke, in the reign of Henry II. The native Irish still held out in the west, but put up little resistance, merely hurling a few stones and spears before rushing back to their forests and swamps. In time many of the English barons began to mix so freely with the Irish that they copied their dress and even their hair-style, having their heads shaved at the front and allowing the rest of their hair to grow long so that

Westminster Hall today. It was begun in the reign of William Rufus, but the wooden roof dates from Richard II's time. It was used for important state occasions, including some parliaments.

it hung down their backs. Only in a small area round Dublin did the English king have much authority.

Edward tried to bring the barons in Ireland under his control by holding a parliament there in 1297. Complaints were heard about bad highways, failure to catch criminals, and those barons who never visited their lands and had all the profits from them sent home to England. Thanks to the peace under Edward's firm rule, more Irish farming villages sprang up and there was an increase in trade which brought wealth to such towns as Dublin and Waterford.

Edward I enthroned in the House of Lords, with Alexander of Scotland on his right and Llewellyn of Wales on his left, to emphasize that he was their overlord. In fact, there was no occasion when all three kings attended Edward's parliament at the same time.

The English in Wales

The native Welsh were a much more dangerous problem than

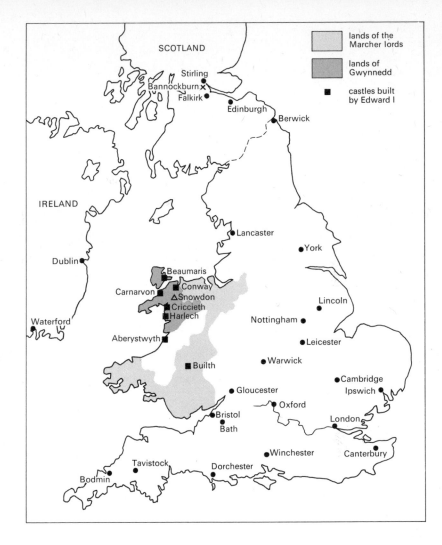

SCOTLAND

Stirling
Bannockburn ✕
Falkirk ●
Edinburgh ●
Berwick ●

IRELAND

Lancaster ●
York ●

Dublin ●

Beaumaris ■
Conway ■
Carnarvon ■ △ Snowdon
Criccieth ■
Harlech ■
Aberystwyth ■

Lincoln ●
Nottingham ●
Leicester ●
Warwick ●

Builth ■

Cambridge ●
Ipswich ●

Gloucester ●
Oxford ●
London
Bristol ●
Bath

Winchester ●
Canterbury ●

Waterford ●

Tavistock ●
Dorchester ●

Bodmin ●

lands of the Marcher lords

lands of Gwynedd

■ castles built by Edward I

Britain at the time of Edward I.

the Irish, who were separated from England by the sea. Before Edward's time, the lords of the Marches or boundary lands had moved west into Wales to carve out great estates for themselves in lowlands and valleys, as you can see from the map. The Welsh retreated into the mountains where they kept their own Celtic language and laws, their kings, and their hatred of the English. The chronicler, Gerald the Welshman, tells us how they would rush down from the hills with wild shrieks, blowing their long war-horns. Yet they were badly armed and if the enemy did not give in at once, they fled in panic.

Llewellyn's revolt

At last the princes of Gwynedd united all the other tribes

under their leadership. They cunningly took the barons' side in their struggle with John and Henry III. As a result, they were able to win back much of Powys from the Marcher lords who were grateful for their help. By Edward's time, Llewellyn, the Prince of Gwynedd, felt strong enough to defy the English king and refused to take an oath of homage to him.

After an attempt to bring the Welsh prince to obedience by seizing his fiancée, Eleanor de Montfort, Earl Simon's daughter, Edward ordered a full-scale invasion. Llewellyn was driven back to his mountain stronghold in Snowdon. Once the grain-growing island of Anglesey was taken by the English, hunger forced him to give in. For a time he remained at peace, but then he and his brother rebelled again; both were killed in the fighting and the last of the Welsh royal family, the little Princess Gwenllian, was brought to England and spent the rest of her life in a convent. A series of castles was built across Wales to discourage further rebellion. Finally, as if to stress his triumph, Edward gave his baby son the title of 'Prince of Wales' at Caernarvon Castle.

Edward's attack on Scotland

Scotland was less likely to accept English rule than Wales or

Harlech Castle in Merionethshire, built under the direction of James, the mason, who had learned the art of castle-building on the Continent. (See the diagram on page 97.)

Ireland. Its kings were well in control of the country and were usually on good terms with the kings of England. All this was changed when Alexander III of Scotland was killed as his horse fell over a cliff. His grand-daughter, Margaret, was his only heir and she died on board the ship bringing her from Norway. As she was to have married Edward's eldest son, this was a blow to English hopes of uniting the two countries peacefully. It came at a time when the English king was stunned by the death of his loyal wife, Eleanor of Castile. His grief was so great that he put up crosses wherever her body rested on the way to London. Charing (sweet-queen) Cross is one of those.

Edward was then given the task of deciding between the twelve men who claimed the Scottish throne. He chose John Balliol and then went on to treat Scotland as a conquered state and Balliol as his servant. When the Scottish king took up arms against him, he was soon defeated. Edward had discovered the power of the longbow in Wales. It could pierce a knight's armour and pin his thigh through the saddle to his horse's side. The new weapon was used with great effect against the Scots.

William Wallace and Scottish resistance

By 1297 it looked as though the war was over. In that year, however, the Scottish knight, William Wallace, began to lead raiding parties over the border. Up to this time the Scots, like the English, had felt little real pride in their country. Their loyalty was rather to their local village and its lord. Wallace's attacks were the first signs of the growth of Scottish patriotism. The spears of the townsmen and peasants whom he led were no match for the

Longbows *(left)* against crossbows. Arrows could be fired in quick succession from the longbow, but crossbows had to be wound up to stretch the cord to high tension *(far right)*.

qui senti sa sante revenue
nuaise entraus·ij· contenue

J lueques trouvast on /les tolereus
c eruevllieres fendues /coutiaus agu

English horsemen. Wallace was defeated at Falkirk and later betrayed to the English. His life might have been saved had he begged for mercy, but he preferred to suffer on the gallows. His body was quartered and his head set up on London Bridge.

Robert Bruce

Still the Scots did not give up. After Balliol's death, Robert Bruce claimed the throne. At first he met only disaster and defeat and he was at one time outlawed by the Church for slitting the throat of his enemy, the Red Comyn, in church. Only four or five days before his death, Edward set out with an army to try to catch him. Once again Bruce escaped and in the reign of Edward's lazy and irresponsible son, Edward II, he went on to win a victory which freed Scotland from all fear of England for years to come. After a night spent in drinking, the finest of the English knights and archers were caught in a bog at Bannockburn and hacked to pieces by the sober Scots.

Edward's failure

Little of Edward's united Britain survived his death, therefore. The Scottish kings, who had freely chosen to copy the language and customs of England in earlier times, became the firm allies of the kings of France for over 200 years. Today in Scotland you can still see castles built in the French style and hear words such as 'tassie' from the French 'tasse' (a cup). In Wales and Ireland the Crown lost control of its barons and peace was at an end. Even in England itself the old quarrel between the king and his barons led once more to civil war. It was not until a Scottish king sat on the English throne that Britain was united under one ruler, not by force but by a common interest.

Edward I's coronation chair which now stands in Westminster Abbey. It encloses the Stone of Scone underneath the seat. Traditionally Scottish kings had been crowned on the Stone, until Edward took it to England in 1296 to support his claim to the Scottish throne.

Dates to remember

1215   Magna Carta was sealed by King John
1265   Simon de Montfort's Parliament
1314   Battle of Bannockburn

Things to do

1   In Edward's time there was a famous saying: 'What concerns all should be approved by all.' How did Edward put this saying into practice?

2 There is a famous story about Robert Bruce being inspired as he watched the spider which kept on rebuilding its web no matter how often it was destroyed. How does this fit in with his real life story?

3 Read *The Ballad of Sir Patrick Spens* – (Anonymous) and *'Scots wha hae wi' Wallace bled'* – (Robert Burns). How far is each one accurate, in fact?

Books to read

L. Stenhouse, *The Story of Scotland*, Benn
M. McCririck, *Stories of Wales*, Book I, E. J. Arnold

A promise made in 1291 by nine of the claimants to the Scottish throne that they would accept Edward's decision. There are only eight seals, because one of them, the Count of Holland, was absent.

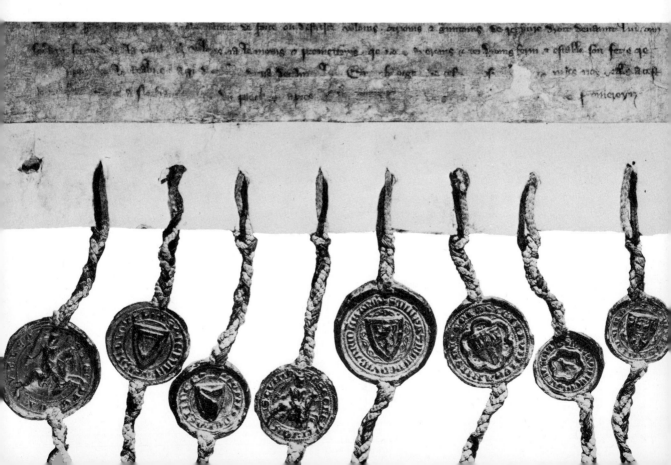

Chapter 11
Life in medieval England

The king and his court

As in Saxon times, it was the king's character which usually decided how much power he should have. Edward I was admired and respected, so that he had little difficulty in making the nobility obey him. His son, Edward II, was weak and unpopular. As a result, he was turned off the throne and murdered by rebel barons.

A king's main duties were still to keep law and order in his realm and to defend it against enemies abroad. He did this with the help of a small council. This included the chancellor, who was in charge of justice and kept all official papers, and the treasurer, who looked after the king's clothes and jewels as well as the money which was paid in taxes to the royal exchequer.

Other royal servants were given the tasks of arranging for the supply and transport of food, drink, horses, dogs and other necessary goods which the king took round with him on his travels from one royal estate to another. For one Christmas feast alone Henry III and his court ate 5000 chickens, 1100 partridges, hares, rabbits, 10,000 eels, 36 swans, 54 peacocks, and 90 boars besides other food such as eggs and cream. To their dismay, villages through which the king passed were often forced to give him extra supplies.

Court of the King's Bench in the fifteenth century. At the top sit the judges; on the left are the jury, being sworn in by an usher; in the foreground, a prisoner stands in the dock, his feet chained together, guarded by a sergeant of the law. Six more prisoners wait their turn.

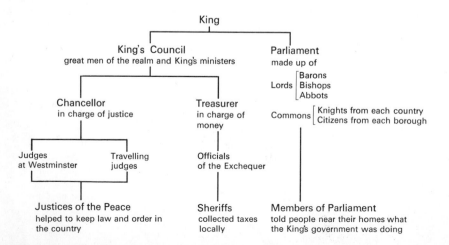

English government in the Middle Ages.

In Edward I's time the exchequer and the courts of law were left at Westminster while the king was on his travels. Royal judges were also sent to tour the country, as they had been doing since the reign of Henry II. These tours are still called 'Assizes', from the French word for 'sittings'. The result of them was that the king's justice was easy for his subjects to find.

Law and justice

People began to take their cases to the royal courts rather than to the court of a local baron because only the king could offer trial by jury. In this, a jury of twelve men decided whether an accused man was innocent or guilty. It was much fairer than trial by ordeal or by battle in which chance played a big part. Also the king's judges and sheriffs were often more honest than those of a local baron who might be too frightened of their master to give a judgement which would offend him.

A monk and lady in the stocks. (Part of the punishment was to suffer the taunts of onlookers.)

Punishments also became more just. Some effort was made to make them fit the crime. A murderer was hanged, or burnt, if a woman. The thief might also be executed, but more likely he would lose the hand with which he stole. The penalty for slandering a neighbour was to have the tongue cut out, while the scolding wife was ducked in a pond or forced to wear a scold's bridle. Some offenders were put in the stocks for the day so that others could pelt them with mud or stones.

As in Saxon times there was no police force and often the victim's only remedy was to hit back on the spot – if he could. Serious crime was even more common than it is today. In Lincoln alone in 1202 there were 114 murders, 89 robberies, and 65 cases of wounding, besides other crimes.

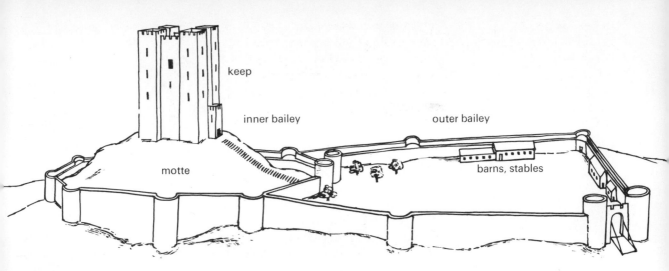

keep

inner bailey

outer bailey

motte

barns, stables

A Norman castle with a square keep. Inside it were sleeping quarters, a large hall, a chapel, a storeroom and dungeons.

The castle

Castles were very important in times of lawlessness because it was possible to control all the countryside for miles around from one of them. Look at the drawing above and you will see that the castle developed from a fortified hill or motte with an enclosed courtyard or bailey in front of it. Later, castles had stronger walls with rounded towers which jutted out so that attackers could not advance under the walls to undermine them without being seen. By the time of Edward I, castles were built on the 'concentric' plan, in which one circular wall enclosed another, as you can see from the photograph on page 98. Usually the only hope of taking a castle of this sort was to besiege it until the defenders ran out of food and water.

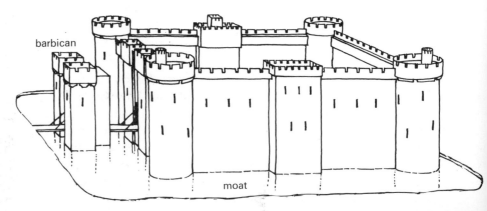

barbican

moat

A fourteenth century castle. The barbican, the two towers at the entrance, was used as an outer defence, guarding the causeway across the moat.

The castle was a most uncomfortable place to live in. Glass was still nearly unknown. Although windows were left as small as possible, draughts blew round the gloomy rooms. The smell from the castle muckheap must have been horrible. The only sanitation was a shaft in the castle walls, which might go down to an underground sewer near the dungeons and the well which was the castle's chief water supply.

Kidwelly Castle, Carmarthenshire, rebuilt in 1270. It has an inner ward with four rounded towers surrounded by an outer wall. The river forms a natural defence for one side of the castle.

How to behave in a castle

Besides the baron and his family the castle might have to house the usual crowd of smiths, armourers, grooms and fighting men who accompanied their lord on his travels. Pages and squires, boys and young men of good family, would also live there. They learnt how to fight and behave themselves in a noble household until the day when they received the spurs of knighthood after a night spent in prayer.

There was a book of instructions which told the squire how to go about his duties. In the morning he was to put his master's clothes to warm by the fire and then:

'. . . draw his socks and hose on by the fire . . .' The illustration is from a book of 1310.

Ask your lord humbly to come to the fire and get dressed by it, and stand by to help him. First, hold out his tunic and his doublet while he puts his arms in, and have his stomacher, stockings and socks well aired so that he does not catch cold and will feel warm for the rest of the day. Then draw his socks and hose on by the fire and fasten up his shoes, pull his hose on well and tie them up to the height he likes, lace his doublet up, and drape a scarf round his shoulders. Then gently comb his hair with an ivory comb and bring water to wash his hands and face. Then kneel down and ask, 'What robe will you wear today, Sir?'

During the day the squire often went hunting with his lord. They might go on foot and send off a falcon which was trained to catch birds and animals and return to its master. At other times they hunted on horseback, sending their hounds after deer, wild

A huntsman blows his horn as his dogs rush forward for the kill.

boar and other animals. They would return to a feast during which the young squire would again have to watch his manners:

When you enter your lord's presence, say 'God speed', and humbly greet all present. Do not rush in rudely, but walk at an even pace with your head held high and kneel before your lord. . . . Don't sit down until you are told to and keep your hands and feet still, not scratching yourself or lounging against a post. . . . Cut your bread with your knife and do not tear it. Use a clean trencher and when the soup is brought, eat it quietly with a spoon and make sure you do not leave it in the dish. Don't lean on the table and make a mess on the cloth or drink with a full mouth. Don't pick your nose, teeth or nails, or take so much into your mouth that you can't answer when anyone speaks to you. When you drink, wipe your mouth and hands clean with a cloth, so that you don't dirty the cup and make your friends unwilling to drink with you.

Sir Geoffrey Luttrell, a knight, at dinner. Food was eaten without forks.

Two medieval entertainments: rehearsing a dancing-bear; a woman balancing on swords to the sound of pipes and a drum.

dieu fait li baudrains / or vos va ricement

on ioulet tuer / au roi qui ne ment uue

Knights tilting. *Above:* the clash of lances; *below:* the result.

After the feast the company might be entertained by travelling jugglers, acrobats and minstrels. Another favourite amusement was the tournament, which was really a mock battle. In this, teams of knights or squires competed against each other or fought in single combat. The object of the contest was to break your opponent's lance or to knock him off his horse. The rules were strict and points were lost for hitting a man when his back was turned or striking his saddle or horse. Even so, death or injury was common. The reward for victory was a present of gold or jewels, or a charger made ready for battle. The lady chosen as the 'queen of Love and Beauty' for the tournament presented the prizes, but each knight wore a glove or some other sign of his lady's favour in his helmet.

The Pastons – a medieval family at home

Because castles were so uncomfortable, some wealthy families chose to live in manor houses, like the one you see above. We know a great deal about one such family, the Pastons, who lived in Norfolk at about the time when Joan of Arc was fighting the English in France. Many of their letters and other papers have come down to us and we can learn much about life in a manor house from them.

Here is a list of the contents of some of their rooms. In the parlour or living-room: one long trestle-table, one short, two forms, one iron plate to hold a candle, one hanging and one piece of tapestry, and one piece of tapestry covering to throw over a bench. In the bedroom (often used as a sitting-room): a feather-bed, a mattress of fine blue, a bolster, two fustian blankets, a pair of sheets, one stitched coverlet, one set of hangings from Arras for the bed, one canopy, one supporting frame, three curtains of green worsted, one piece of tapestry for throwing over a bench, fire tongs and bellows, one little pallet, two blankets, one pair of sheets, one coverlet, six cushions, one trestle-table, one long chair, one hanging candlestick, two little bells. In the kitchen: two dozen pewter dishes, three pots of brass, two spits,

Haddon Hall, Derbyshire. Parts of it are Norman, but the Vernon family, who came to own it, enlarged it and made it much more comfortable in the fourteenth and fifteenth centuries. Although built as a manor-house, it still looks like a castle.

Plan of a medieval manor house.

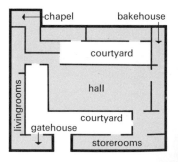

From a medieval kitchen: a decorated pitcher (thirteenth century); a bronze cooking-pot used by the well-to-do (fourteenth century); a cook's flesh-hook for picking out the contents of a boiling cauldron (see page 105); and a pair of shears, more commonly used than scissors.

one mortar and pestle, two pothooks, two skewers, one wood-axe, four great brass pans, one gridiron, one dressing knife, two iron rakes, one meat safe, six tablecloths, six towels, six pewter candlesticks, two silver salts, two pewter salts, a stool, two pewter basins and jugs, one barrel of vinegar, twelve ale stands, two pantry knives, one piece of silver plate, twelve silver spoons.

Marriage and a woman's work

Although the poor might marry whom they chose, richer families arranged marriages which would bring money and lands to the family. Often the couple were only introduced to each other when their parents had already arranged the date of their wedding. Girls were married at twelve or even younger.

Most of the marriages arranged in the Paston family worked

Comforts of the fifteenth century: a fireplace and panelled walls to keep in the warmth.

out very well. Margery Paston, however, fell in love with her father's bailiff, Richard Calle. In one letter he wrote begging her to tell her family that they were engaged:

I suppose if ye tell them the truth, they would not damn their souls for us. Though I tell them the truth, they will not believe me as well as they will you. And therefore, good lady, at the reverence of God, be plain to them and tell them the truth. . . . I pray you let no creature see this letter. . . . Almighty Jesu preserve, keep and give you your heart's desire. . . . This letter was written with as great pain as ever I wrote anything in my life.

At last, after having been bullied for months by her family, Margery was allowed to marry Richard, for the Pastons could find no way of breaking their betrothal which was as binding as a marriage in those days.

Once married, a woman was supposed to obey her husband in all things and disobedient wives were often beaten. As in Saxon times her duty was to cook food for the family and to keep the house in good order. She might do the spinning or weaving herself or buy material for the family's clothes from a nearby town. Some garments could be bought ready made.

Fashionable hair-styling in 1340. The maid holds up a mirror.

Shopping lists

The Paston women did not travel far from home, but when the men went to some big town, they were given detailed instructions about what to buy there. One Paston was told to:

Buy me three yards of purple, price to the yard 4s., a bonnet of deep plum-colour, price 2s. 4d., a hose cloth of yellow-ribbed cloth – about an ell – I trow it will cost 2s., a girdle of plum-coloured ribbon, price 6d., three pair of wooden thick-soled shoes – I was used to paying 2½d. for a pair – but I pray you let them not be left behind though I pay more. They must be low; let them be long enough and broad at the heel.

Food

Wealthy families in the Middle Ages seem to have eaten more food than we should consider necessary today. For breakfast in Lent, when no meat was eaten, a guest of the Pastons was expected to eat: a loaf of bread, a quart of beer, a dish of butter, a piece of salt-fish, a dish of sprats or three white herring. At one of their feasts the poor were given soup, boiled beef, and roast pork. As a first course the other guests had chicken broth, fowl, mutton, geese and custard. The second course was a hotch-potch

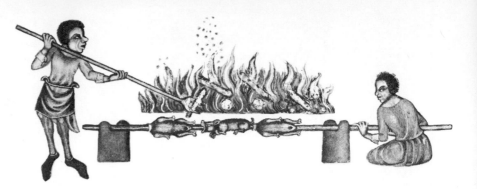

Roasting sucking-pig and fowl on a spit.

of meat and herbs, fowl, lamb, pork, veal, roasted pigeons, baked rabbits, pheasants, venison, jelly, and other delicacies.

The cooks of the Middle Ages must have been highly skilled, for they prepared food which had to look as good as it tasted. They used many spices, partly, no doubt, to cover the taste of meat which had been kept through the winter. We know of many recipes which were used in the Pastons' time. Some of them, such as the one for the peacock which has to be skinned, roasted on a spit, and then arranged on a dish with his feathers so that he looked alive, we would not use today. Other recipes are for simpler dishes, such as an omelette, which was made much as it is now. Here is how the Pastons might have made a fruit tart:

Take figs and boil them in wine and grind them small. . . . Put them in a vessel and add thereto powder pepper, cannell, cloves, mace, powder ginger, great raisins, saffron and salt. Then make a fair, low coffin (pastry case) and put this stuff therein. Put thereto cut dates and fresh salmon in fair pieces or else fresh eels and boil them in a little wine. Cover the coffin with the same paste and put into the oven to bake.

Left: the cook inspects the dinner; *right:* meat and poultry are chopped up before serving.

A villein's life

You will have noticed that the poor men at the Pastons' feast were given much simpler food than the other guests. Even this must have been a treat for them. Since the only animals which most villeins kept were one or two cows (to give milk) and a pig, they rarely had any meat except a little bacon. Potatoes had not yet come to England so they lived mostly on bread, cheese, vegetables and any fish, rabbit or hare or other animal or bird which could be caught. The forest usually belonged to some great lord and there were heavy penalties for poaching, so that the villein had to keep much of his hunting secret.

In the drawing of a medieval village on the opposite page you will see that the villeins' huts are set along the village street. Each one had a small garden or croft in which vegetables were grown and chickens reared. The cottage itself might be a one-roomed shack made of mud and stones with a hole in the roof to let the smoke out. Better houses were made of a wooden frame, like the one in the drawing, with walls of mud and straw plastered on to basketwork of wattle. The roof was thatched with straw and the floor was of earth trodden hard. On rainy days the water would ooze through it into the cottage. Water had to be fetched from the village well.

The villein's dark, smelly little house would be shared by his wife, children, and possibly some chickens and a pig or two, though these wandered on the common in day-time. The only furniture would be a trestle-table and one or two stools. The family might use home-carved wooden bowls, plates and spoons at meal-times. They slept on mattresses of straw or twigs, gathered from the common, in the clothes they wore during the day.

A cow licks her calf while she is being milked.

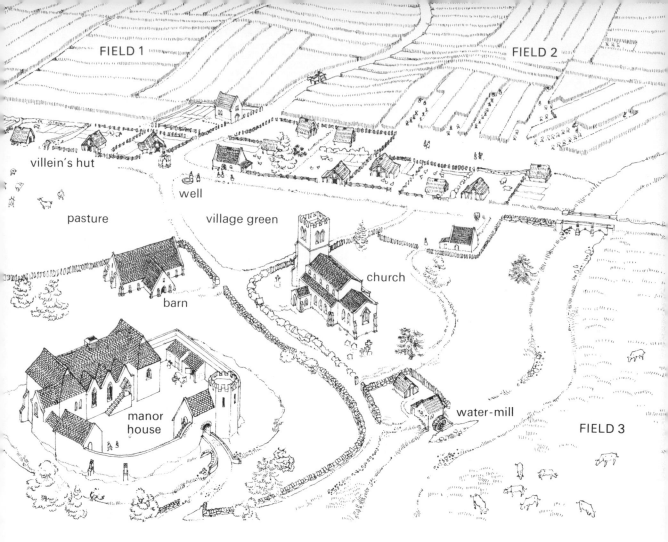

FIELD 1

FIELD 2

villein's hut

well

pasture

village green

church

barn

manor
house

water-mill

FIELD 3

A medieval village. Like
Saxon villages, it is
surrounded by three fields.

Building one of the better
kind of villeins' houses.
Compare it with the Saxon
huts on page 32.

Scything grass; netting fish; beating down acorns to feed pigs; and bringing grapes to a vat, where they are trodden down and the juice crushed out. Wine was made in England during the Middle Ages, but most people preferred French wine when it could be imported.

iudicia tua domine
Quoniam tu dominus altiffin
super omnem terram: nimis exa
tus es super omnes deos.

Above: carting hay up a steep hill. *Below:* an old peasant woman takes her corn to be ground at the local windmill.

Outwardly the life of a poor man had changed little since Saxon times. Throughout the centuries he went on with the tasks of ploughing, muckspreading, hedging, ditching and sheep-shearing according to the time of year. His wife busied herself with household tasks or did light work about the manor, such as churning butter and cheese, brewing beer, or gleaning in the cornfield.

After the coming of the Normans, however, the Saxon churls were no longer free men who could find another lord if they chose. The duties which they had to perform in return for their land became even heavier. They were expected to work three days a week on the demesne (the lord's land), with extra labour called boon work at times such as harvest when more help was needed. They gave gifts of fowls, eggs and pigs to their lord and paid to use his mill, ovens and wine-press. The village priest could also claim a tithe (tenth) of the villeins' produce, which would be kept in the tithe barn. If they had some complaint against the lord and his men, the case was heard in the manor court in which the lord or his sheriff acted as judge. Any villein who tried to run away was flogged and might have his tongue or ears cut off. In his absence his family might be left to starve.

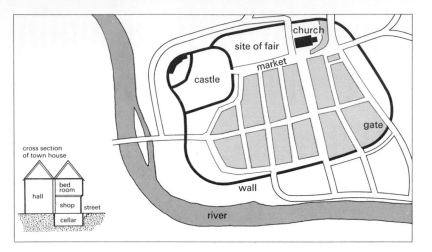

Labels in image: church, site of fair, market, castle, gate, wall, gate, river

cross section of town house — hall, bed room, shop, street, cellar

Plan of a medieval town.

The towns

Any villein who reached a town and stayed there for a year and a day without being caught became a free man. During the Middle Ages the towns grew in population and importance. London was still by far the greatest city in England with York and Bristol next in order of size. You can see from the above plan that the town was often walled for defence and that the houses and shops were laid out neatly in square blocks with streets running between. Many towns had their own government after buying freedom from their overlords. A mayor and aldermen were chosen from among the richer citizens. Their duties included keeping law and order, sharing out food in time of

Left: sawing a plank. *Below:* cloth is dyed in a heated vat.

Builders and stonemasons: they plane the top layer of bricks flat and check its vertical angle with a plumbline; the man on the ladder is using a drill, and two others below prepare the stone.

shortage, arranging drainage and water supply, seeing that the streets were kept clear of rubbish and the air clear of coal smoke.

Those engaged in each trade or craft tended to live together in one part of the town. Names such as Fish Street or the Corn-market give us a clue to what was sold there during the Middle Ages. Among the craftsmen and traders might be smiths, carpenters, wheelwrights, coopers, tilers, goldsmiths, leather-workers, glovers, weavers, fullers, dyers, tailors, millers, cooks, bakers, butchers and mercers (drapers). Many English surnames show that someone in the family once earned his living by one of these crafts.

The guild

The masters of each craft belonged to a guild. By its rules a youth was to spend seven years as an apprentice learning the necessary

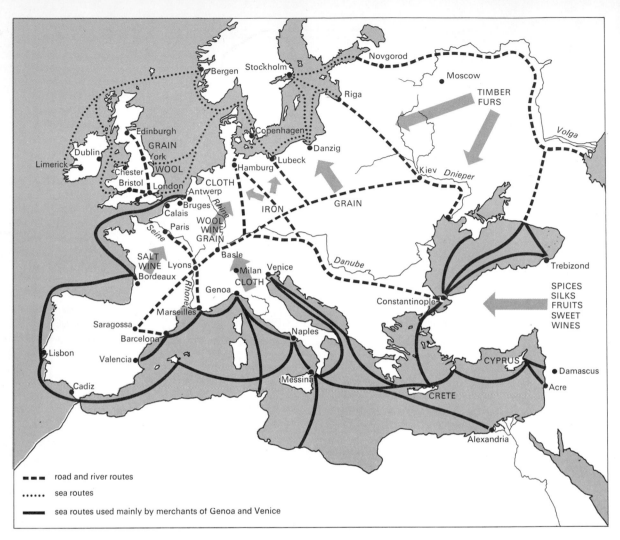

Trade routes and trade in medieval Europe.

A customer choosing a mirror.

skill. During this time he was to live with his master's family. When his training was finished, he took a test. If he passed it, he became a journeyman and was paid by the day for his work. Some journeymen managed to save up enough to set up in business for themselves and become masters. They did this by allowing the other guild members to inspect the best example of their work – the 'masterpiece'.

The guild also laid down rules about the quality and price of goods. When a master became ill, the other members of the guild would help him or look after his wife and children if he died. Some of the guild's money went to build chapels or schools. On feast days of the Church the different crafts acted stories from the Bible and so began the theatre in England.

Markets and fairs

Trade and the use of money greatly increased at the time of the crusades when men travelled out to the East and saw the silks and spices to be bought there. Traders in English towns sold most of their goods at the weekly markets. At these, people from the surrounding countryside brought in their farm produce and exchanged it for goods made in the town.

Once a year, however, a fair would take place at important centres like Cambridge or in villages near the capital. Mayfair was one of these. Merchants from as far away as France and Germany came to sell luxuries such as wines or fine cloth and ribbons in exchange for English wool, tin, lead, coal and iron. Stalls with tented roofs were put up to house the traders and entertainers who helped to keep the crowd amused. There was even a travelling dentist who pulled out bad teeth for a small fee.

A Flemish market in the late fifteenth century. Similar markets were held in England.

A Punch and Judy show in 1340. Punch does not seem to have changed since.

Learning and education

As in Saxon times there were schools at monasteries and cathedrals, but many towns now had their own grammar schools. The boys who went there learnt how to read, write and speak Latin, which was the language used by teachers and writers throughout Europe. Books were scarce, for before the invention of printing they all had to be copied out by hand. Pupils had to learn much of their work by heart and were harshly beaten if they made a mistake or did not pay attention in class. Among the offences for which boys of Westminster School could be punished were not washing properly, fighting, giggling and scuffling in church, being rude, swearing, and having pillow fights at bed-time.

Some boys went on to the schools at Oxford and Cambridge which became famous as centres of learning where the best teachers could be found. There they studied such subjects as arithmetic, music, geometry, astronomy, law, medicine, and theology. Many did not stay the four years needed to get a degree, and those who went on to one of the colleges for more advanced study had to enter the Church and were not allowed to marry. Chaucer gives us this picture of one thin, poorly dressed clerk of Oxford:

Merton College, Oxford, founded in 1264. It was one of the first colleges to be built; the hall *(left)* and one quadrangle *(extreme left)* date from the thirteenth century.

For rather would he have at his bed's head
Twenty books clad in black and red,
Of Aristotle and his philosophy,
Than rich robes, fiddle or merry salter.
For all that he was a philosopher
He had little gold in his coffer . . .
Of study he took most care and heed.
Not a word spoke he more than was need.

Most students at the universities came from quite wealthy families like the Pastons or from the merchant class in the towns. Still, some villeins did manage to get permission from their lords to leave the village to study. Often they were helped by the local parish priest. The only English Pope, Adrian IV, whose real name was Nicholas Breakspear, showed that it was possible to rise from the humblest beginnings to a position of great power even in the Middle Ages. Girls, of course, had no such chance and were kept at home or sent off to some great house to learn how to behave. However, the Paston women knew how to read and write and it seems likely that other ladies of high birth did too.

Education. Beside the sketch is a verse: 'Wisdom that is not willingly sought, With the rod must needs be taught.'

A scientific revolution

Medieval people were slowly becoming more interested in the world around them. When European scholars began to visit centres of learning in Moslem and Byzantine lands at the time of the crusades, they discovered works by Greek writers which had been lost during the barbarian invasions in the West. The most important of these were Aristotle's books on science, for they led scholars to study the evidence before them much more closely and to make up their own minds about it instead of believing all that they had been told by the great men of the past.

This change is shown in the work of Adelard of Bath, a great scientist who worked for William the Conqueror's youngest son, Henry I, and travelled much abroad, usually wearing a green cloak. One of his books is in the form of a talk between Adelard and his nephew, a rather dull young man who asks,

'If you dig up dry earth and sieve it and put it into a pot of earthenware or bronze, who else but God will cause plants to spring up from it?' Adelard replied, 'I do not wish to claim that God is less than all-powerful. But nature has its own pattern and order and we should pay attention to those who have learnt something of it. Only when they fail should we bring God into it.'

115

A cripple seeking aid from the church. In the Middle Ages, anyone who could not work had to beg.

For a time in the thirteenth and early fourteenth centuries, English scientists led all Europe. Most of them worked at Oxford, where the friar, Roger Bacon, did experiments with light, heat and magnetism. William of Ockham studied falling objects and so paved the way for the work of Galileo and Newton, who much later discovered the laws of gravity. William Merlee was one of the first men in the Middle Ages to keep careful records of the weather and even tried to forecast it in advance by noting such signs as the lively jumping of fleas which showed that there was moisture in the air. Sometimes life could be dangerous for the scientist. Roger Bacon was imprisoned on a charge that he had called up the devil because he had been experimenting with gunpowder and his room stank of sulphur.

Although the Church frowned on the dissection of dead bodies by doctors who wanted to study them, medical knowledge also increased. One famous physician, John of Arderne, wrote a book in which he advises cleanliness and a solemn manner which will inspire faith in the patient, just as we would today. He describes one case of a fisherman who had pierced his arm on an iron spike. The wound had been clumsily dressed by a barber and had gone septic. This was Arderne's treatment:

After removing the old bandage I applied a light ointment and oil of roses. Before cockcrow the patient was free from aching and the swelling was beginning to go down. In the morning he was sleeping soundly and the pus had left the wound. Note that I used no dressing. . . .

No doubt the fisherman would need all his strength to face Arderne's bill when he woke up, for the great doctor rarely

Opposite page:

Top: Treating the sick in the early thirteenth century. At the apothecary's (chemist's) shop, herbs from the table are weighed, pounded up, and heated over a fire.

Centre: One patient *(left)* inhales healing fumes, while another consults the doctor about his skin disease (probably impetigo).

Bottom left: the surgeon decides where to cut. *Bottom right:* the operation in progress. One assistant holds the patient down; the other demands the fee.

charged less than one hundred shillings for a serious case and often a great deal more if he thought his patient could afford it.

Interest in science was not just limited to a few learned men. We find the poet Chaucer writing a book to explain to his little son Lewis how to use an astrolabe, like the one which you see on this page, as a guide to the position of the planets and the stars. As life grew more dangerous and difficult in the fifteenth century, the people had less wish to study the world about them. More use was made of machinery such as water-mills, geared wheels and lathes, but the scientific revolution died away before it led to inventions of real importance.

Astronomers using astrolabes and nocturnals to calculate the movement of the stars.

Change in the Middle Ages

During the 300 years after the Norman Conquest, conditions in which the people lived and worked changed little. Styles in dress and architecture came and went, but the lives of the villein in the manor and even the craftsman in the town remained the same. It needed a horrible plague at home and a disastrous war abroad to change the face of medieval England.

Dates to remember

about 1249   University College founded at Oxford
      1386   Chaucer began to write the *Canterbury Tales*
about 1420   The Paston letters begin

Things to do

1   Try to discover a castle or manor house near your home. Compare it with the ones on pages 97 and 98.
2   Make a list of the furniture in the living-room, bedroom and kitchen of your home. Compare it with what the Pastons owned, remembering that they were a wealthy family.
3   Look at the prices on Mrs Paston's shopping list. Try to find the cost of similar things today.
4   Work out a menu of the day's food, first for a lord's family and then for a villein's family.
5   Did your local town exist in the Middle Ages? If so, try to discover how much of the old walls and street plan remains, and whether the old church or school is still standing.
6   Find out what you can about Pope Adrian IV, Roger Bacon, William of Ockham, and Geoffrey Chaucer.

Books to read

Christine Price, *Made in the Middle Ages*, Bodley Head
M. and C. H. B. Quennell, *A History of Everyday Things in England*, Book I: 1066–1499, Batsford
Alfred Duggan, *Growing up in the Thirteenth Century*, Faber
E. Osmond, *Towns*, Batsford
Agnes Allen, *The Story of Clothes*, Faber

Stealing cherries.

Chapter 12
Joan of Arc and the Hundred Years War

How the Hundred Years War began

After Edward II's defeat at Bannockburn there followed years of struggle between the king and his barons. Finally Edward was murdered. His son, Edward III, proved to be a capable and popular king. As the country became more peaceful and prosperous under his rule, he began to look for the chance to extend his power abroad. The horrors of war did not frighten Edward. Instead he looked forward to the time when his nobles would be kept busy fighting abroad instead of being bored and restless at home.

England's natural enemy seemed to be her neighbour, France. As you can see from the map, the English kings still had some lands in France. Also Edward's mother was a French princess and this gave him the excuse to claim that he was the rightful king of France in 1337. The French preferred Philip of Valois and argued that under an old law no woman could have any claim to the French throne. So Edward began preparations for war. His people were only too anxious to support him. They were annoyed by the way the French had used their influence to stop the cloth merchants of Flanders from buying English wool. Bad feeling was also caused by French pirates who attacked ships carrying wine from Gascony to England.

English victory and French resistance

At first the French army, which was made up of a few Swiss crossbowmen and a large force of cavalry and men-at-arms fighting on foot, was no match for the longbowmen of England. The first great English victory was won at Crécy in 1346. As you can see from the plan, the two armies were drawn up near a forest. The French knights showed more courage than sense by charging into the attack before the word of command had been given. They trampled down their own archers in their efforts to reach the enemy. As they approached the English lines, they were met by a hail of arrows. Those who came through this were nearly all cut down by the knights who waited on foot to protect the archers. The English won without even having to move from their positions and their losses were small. It was in this battle

Battle lines at Crécy.

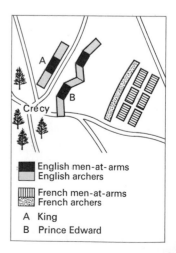

English men-at-arms
English archers

French men-at-arms
French archers

A King
B Prince Edward

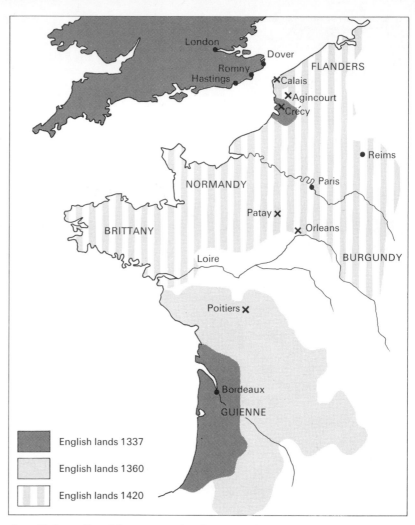

English possessions in France during the Hundred Years War. The lands won in 1360 were lost soon after. By the end of the fifteenth century, all that remained of the English lands in France was a small area round Calais.

English lands 1337

English lands 1360

English lands 1420

that Edward's eldest son, the Prince of Wales, first showed his bravery. Before his early death from a disease caught on campaign he won other victories and was much hated by the French for his cruelty. Later he became known as 'the Black Prince', probably because of the colour of his armour.

Slowly the French realized that they must change their tactics. A new general, Du Guesclin, saw that the English army could not move quickly enough to escape when surprised. It was unbeatable only when the French were so unwise as to attack it after it had taken up position. Du Guesclin therefore avoided battle unless the English were taken unawares. He concentrated instead on taking castles in English hands by the skilful use of gunpowder and cannon. In 1396 Richard II, the Black Prince's son, ended the costly and unsuccessful war and made peace.

The triumph of Henry V

The French success was not to last. King Charles VI of France went mad. The powerful Duke of Burgundy tried to seize power from him and went over to the English side when he failed. Richard II died mysteriously – probably killed on the orders of his cousin, Henry IV, who replaced him on the throne. The new king did not feel safe enough to begin war with France again, but his son, Henry V, landed in Normandy in 1415. On the field of Agincourt the French made their old mistake of charging the enemy head-on and were badly defeated by a smaller army suffering from hunger and disease. Seven thousand Frenchmen and 400 Englishmen died. The battle was followed by a treaty in which it was agreed that any son of Henry and the French princess, Katherine, who became his wife, should rule both

The field of Agincourt. The English, wearing the cross of St George, in combat with French knights.

Henry V. The portrait is probably based on an earlier one, painted during the king's lifetime.

A study of Charles VII by Fouquet, an outstanding French painter.

England and France. Charles the Dauphin, the real heir to the French throne, was not allowed to succeed to his kingdom.

Joan's meeting with the Dauphin

Soon after the treaty was made, Henry V died and so did the mad, old King of France. Although Henry's heir was only a baby, the English still seemed to be in a strong position. Even his mother had disowned the Dauphin Charles. He appeared spineless and stupid. He did claim the throne, but without money he could do little. He was defeated in the country to the south of the Loire, one of the few areas still loyal to him. Worst of all, the city of Orleans was besieged by the English and likely to fall to them. It seemed that only a miracle could prevent France being completely taken over by the English and it was at this point that Joan of Arc came forward to save her country.

We can let Joan begin her own story as she told it to the judges at her trial:

I was born in the village of Domrémy. My father is Jacques d'Arc and my mother is Isabeau. When I was thirteen, I had a message from our Lord telling me how to behave myself. The first time I was very frightened. The voice came to me about noon in my father's garden. It seemed to come from the direction of the church and usually it was very clear. After I heard it three or four times, I knew it was the voice of an angel. The voice told me two or three times a week that I must leave and come to France without my father knowing. The voice told me to come to France and I could stay where I was no longer.

So Joan set out to meet Robert de Beaudricourt, the commander of troops in a nearby town. At their first meeting he ordered her to be sent off home with a good smack. After seeing her for the third time he agreed to help her reach the Dauphin, saying, 'Go, go, and come what will.'

Joan described her meeting with the Dauphin in these words:

After dinner I went to my king in the castle. . . . When I came into the king's room, I recognized him from among the others on the advice of my voice.

After a short talk with Joan, a smile was seen to brighten the Dauphin's sulky face. Soon she set out, dressed in boy's clothing, to begin her task of saving France from the English at Orleans.

The rescue of Orleans

Rumours of the coming of 'the Maid', as Joan was now called,

reached the city. Its people took fresh heart and greeted her when she arrived as 'one of the angels of God'. She sent a defiant message to the English which ended:

Siege of a town in the fifteenth century. English armies began to use cannons during the Hundred Years War.

I will make such trouble for you as you will never forget. This is what I am writing to you and I shall not write again.

She carried out her threat by leading an attack on an English stronghold against the advice of leading French generals. With Joan in command the French fought so fiercely that the English were badly shaken. Only a week after her arrival they retreated from Orleans.

Victory and disaster

Joan's next aim was to get the Dauphin crowned at Reims. None of the royal advisers would agree, for the city was in the middle of lands belonging to Charles' great enemy, the Duke of Burgundy. The Dauphin, however, sided with Joan. He still had little money, but so great was the fame of the Maid that men flocked to join her army. At Patay the French had their revenge for Agincourt when 2000 Englishmen died at the cost of only a few French lives. The Burgundian cities gave in all along the way. In July 1429, Joan saw Charles VII crowned at Reims.

Almost at once he took control of the fighting himself and put his trust in those advisers who were most jealous of the Maid. After a half-hearted attempt to take Paris he disbanded most of his army. Joan was given no work of importance to do. Less than a year after the coronation she was taken prisoner by the Burgundians and handed over to the English who arranged for the Church to try her as a heretic, someone who held beliefs contrary to the teaching of the Church. Her king did nothing to save her.

The trial of a saint

Much to their surprise, the judges at her trial found it very hard to prove anything against Joan. Her sharp wits and sense of fun defeated her learned accusers at every point. Here are a few of her answers:

Question   How did St Michael look when he appeared to you? Was he naked?
Answer   Do you think God had no clothes for him?
Question   Does God hate the English?
Answer   About that I know nothing, but I do know they will be driven out of France.
Question   Did your hope of victory rest on your standard or on your sword?
Answer   It lay in our Lord and nowhere else.

The only drawing of Joan made during her lifetime was this sketch in the margin of a document which recounts the relief of Orleans.

At last the threat of torture and the arguments of her judges persuaded Joan to deny that her voice came from God and to submit to the orders of the Church. She put on women's clothing again, but the evil attentions of her jailers forced her to return to boy's dress. This was taken as a sign of disobedience and Joan was condemned to death.

Joan's death

As she made her last speech before being burned even the English wept. Eye-witnesses tell us that,

She asked to have a cross and an English soldier who stood near made a little one of two pieces of wood. He held it up to her at the end of a stick and she took it reverently and kissed it and put it near her breast. She pleaded that I go and fetch the crucifix from a nearby church and hold it before her eyes until her death. . . . Even while in the flames she continued to call out and confess the Blessed Name of Jesus.

The spirit of French patriotism which Joan roused did not die with her. By 1453 the war was over and only Calais was in English hands. Some agree with the Church that she was a saint. Others see in her voices a sign that she was mad or had a disease of the brain. Whatever the truth, she is important as an example of the power of religion and love of country in men's minds. As they

Joan at the stake.

fought the French, the English also began to feel patriotism and loyalty to their country and its king instead of just to their local town or village and its lord.

Dates to remember

1337   Edward III claimed the French throne
1415   The English triumphed at Agincourt
1429   Joan's victory at Orleans
1453   The Hundred Years War ended

Things to do

1   Study the plan of the battle of Agincourt and see how it agrees with what you know of the tactics of the two sides during the Hundred Years War.

2   What do you think is meant by a saint? How far does Joan fit in with your ideas?

3   There have been many plays and films about Joan. Two of the most famous are by Shaw (*St Joan*), and by Shakespeare (*King Henry VI*, Part I). Read some scenes from them and compare their different opinions of Joan.

4   During the Hundred Years War the great French historian, Froissart, wrote:

The English will never love or honour their king, unless he is victorious and loves fighting. They war against their neighbours, especially those who are richer than themselves; their land is wealthier when they are at war than when they are at peace. They thoroughly enjoy battles and slaughter and they are always jealous of other people's riches.

Discuss whether this is still true today.

Books to read

R. E. Oakshott, *A Knight and his Weapons*, Lutterworth
E. Kyle, *Maid of Orleans, Joan of Arc*, Nelson (Picture Biography Series)
E. Doorly, *The Story of France*, Cape

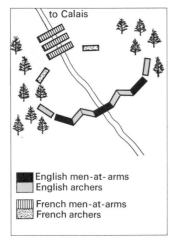

to Calais

■ English men-at-arms
□ English archers

▥ French men-at-arms
▦ French archers

Battle lines at Agincourt.

Chapter 13
Wat Tyler and the Peasants' Revolt

A time of change

While the English soldiers were fighting in France, great changes were taking place at home. As you read earlier, the life of the poor was hard in the Middle Ages. The poet William Langland tells us,

> Whatever they earn at weaving all goes on rent
> Instead of porridge or milk and meal
> To feed the babes who howl for food.
> Hungry they rise at night in bitter, wintry cold
> To rock the cradle in a tiny room.

Yet you can tell from this poem that villeins were beginning to earn wages for farmwork or spinning, instead of working for nothing but a few strips of land on the manor. As money was commonly used in buying and selling, it became easier to pay wages and rents in money too. At the same time villeins were able to earn more because there was a shortage of workers, for about one-third of England's people had died of a new and terrible disease.

The Black Death

Early death was common in medieval times. Many children died from starvation or disease and forty was considered a ripe old age. As you have read, doctors knew little of the human body, and many of their cures were little more than magic spells. When a plague which had spread across Europe from the East reached

Burning clothes of the victims of the Black Death, to stop the spread of the infection.

A procession of monks scourging themselves in the hope of warding off the plague which they believed to be God's punishment for sin. This painting is from Flanders, but scenes in England were probably very similar.

England in 1348, there was little chance of stopping it. At first it was carried by fleas living on black rats which travelled on board ship, but later it was spread direct from one infected person to another. Sometimes the Black Death, as it was called, carried off its victims in a few hours. Others lingered on for days or weeks. Few who caught it survived.

So many died that the harvest rotted in the fields, for there was no one to gather it in. Prices went down, for people no longer cared for riches or property when tomorrow they might be dead. A horse could be had for 6s. 8d., an ox for 4s., a cow for a shilling, a sheep for threepence, a lamb for twopence, and a large pig for fivepence. At the same time, lords began to pay high wages – as much as tenpence a day with meals – to those villeins who had escaped the plague. Some even tried to lure workers from neighbouring manors with the promise of more money. In this way many peasants gained their freedom and better conditions for their families than they had known before.

Others were not so lucky. Their lords forced them to perform every possible task in return for their land, and dragged them back when they ran away. Parliament, which was largely made up of landowners, passed new laws to keep wages and prices down.

Never before had villeins had such an opportunity to make money and yet their lords would not allow them to take advantage of it.

> Now they'll accept no penny-ale, no piece of bacon,
> They must have meat and fish, well fried or baked,
> They must be richly paid or else they rage
> And curse the King and all his council too
> Who make such laws which hurt the working man.

Friars and priests who preached revolt

The poorer clergy agreed with the complaints of the villeins. Some Franciscan friars, whom you read about on page 65, had become rich and idle, but some made no secret of their sympathy for the poor and encouraged them to be discontented. Other priests listened to the ideas of John Wycliffe, a master of Oxford University, who criticized the Church and the Pope. One of his followers, John Ball, went further and compared the simple life of Jesus on earth to the wealth and luxury which great churchmen enjoyed. He pointed to the great contrast between the easy life of the rich and the miseries of those who worked for them and asked,

> When Adam delved (dug) and Eve span,
> Who was then the gentleman?

Ball and the other Lollards, meaning 'babblers', as the followers of Wycliffe came to be called, even suggested that it might be right to kill the great lords of the kingdom and all who supported them, if they did not govern justly.

The rebels find a leader

Revolt finally broke out when the government tried to pay for its unsuccessful wars against France by a poll tax. In 1381 collectors came round to take three groats, a shilling, from everyone over the age of fifteen. The tax was particularly unfair, for the richest man in England, John of Gaunt, the king's uncle, paid no more than the poorest villein. Many villagers went into hiding rather than pay and feeling ran so high that tax-collectors were beaten up in Kent and Essex. Groups of angry peasants began to gather and move towards London. When the men of Kent reached Maidstone, they chose Wat Tyler as their leader. We know little about him except that he was said to be *a man of great cunning and common sense*. He probably came from Kent or Essex. He may have been a soldier or even a man of noble family, but it is just as

'Adam delved and Eve span.' John Ball's words were easily understood by his audience because paintings like this were common in medieval churches.

John Ball riding with his followers. Wat Tyler *(left)* leads another group to join him. Both parties carry the royal standard and the cross of St George, to show their loyalty to the king.

likely that he was a craftsman or labourer with the power to lead men and sway them with his words.

The fall of London

Under Tyler's command the rebels covered the seventy miles between Canterbury and Blackheath in only two days. The king, Richard II, was only fifteen years old and took refuge in the Tower with the treasurer, Hales, and Archbishop Sudbury, who were both blamed by the peasants for the poll tax. Tyler and his men kept stressing that they were loyal to the king. It was his

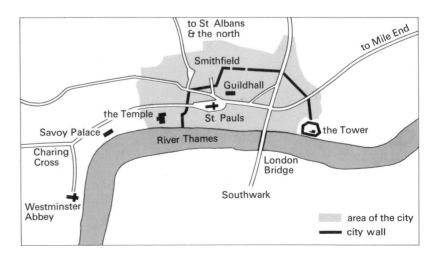

Plan of London in 1371.

advisers they blamed. Yet when Richard came by barge to meet them, they appeared so threatening that it was not thought safe for the king to land.

The peasants then stormed into London through gates which had been left open by the timid citizens. They burned all the records they could find, for they thought these might be used to prove that some men were villeins. Then Tyler led them to John of Gaunt's palace of the Savoy. They destroyed it completely with the aid of gunpowder. So great was Tyler's control over his men that nothing was stolen. The rebels claimed they were not thieves. They wanted only justice. One man who disobeyed orders and took a silver piece was thrown into the flames at once.

The meeting at Mile End

The king then shouted down to the rebels who were gathered outside the Tower that he would meet them the next day at Mile End. As he arrived, the peasants knelt and cried 'Welcome, King Richard, we want you only for our king.' Richard agreed to their demands that all men should be free, that they should be allowed to earn the best wages they could get, and that they should pay only fourpence an acre in rent for their land. Most of the men of Essex went home after this.

Meanwhile other rebels who were not at the meeting had broken into the Tower, although it was supposed to be guarded by over a thousand men. Hales and the old white-haired archbishop were dragged out to be beheaded. The king's mother was rudely treated by the peasants, but escaped unharmed and joined her son who had been wandering through the city almost alone in the confusion. The next day he rode out to face Tyler and the men of Kent at Smithfield.

The king in command

The rebels' demands were much the same as they had been at Mile End, except that they suggested that the lands of the Church should be seized and that there should only be one bishop. Yet Tyler's manner was very different from what it had been before. He refused to take his hat off in the king's presence and, feeling thirsty, he rinsed his mouth out with beer and spat it out on the ground very rudely. The Mayor of London, Walworth, could bear it no longer and lost his temper. Tyler tried to draw his sword, but Walworth managed to wound him. As he tried to spur his horse towards his followers, he was pulled down and killed by a squire called Standish.

The death of the archbishop and treasurer. (This miniature dates from a century after the event and some of its details are wrong.)

Two scenes at Smithfield involving the king. *Left:* Walworth strikes Tyler down; *right:* the king rides up to the peasants to lead them away.

The other rebels could not really see what was going on. They might easily have turned against Richard and his party and murdered them on the spot. The young king showed amazing courage and presence of mind by riding forward and crying, 'Sirs, will you shoot your king? I am your leader. Follow me.' Meekly they did as he asked and he led them out of London and sent them off to their homes with a free pardon.

Soon the council, led by his uncles, made him change his mind. Only a few weeks later Richard told a group of peasants from Essex, 'Villeins you are and villeins you will stay.' The remaining leaders of the revolt, including John Ball, were all tried and executed. Still, the government's revenge could have been worse. Few were tortured and many who were guilty managed to get off. We only hear of a few examples of real cruelty like that at

St Albans where the rebels who had attacked the abbey were hung in chains to make their sufferings worse.

Freedom for the peasants

The king and his councillors never forgot the revolt. They had been the first in England to feel the strength of ordinary labourers who had been roused to anger and found leaders able to guide them. There was still some attempt to keep wages down, but the hated poll tax never returned. In time the shortage of workers forced even the strictest of lords to pay wages. Slowly, the peasants began to win the freedom to choose their masters and to get the best wages they could from them. There were no more villeins left in England.

The rest of the nation felt the effects of these changes. Instead of granting land to their followers, the great noblemen came to pay out money to those who were willing to serve them. Loyalty was sold for gold. Soon local wars broke out between groups of men hired by rival lords.

The Wars of the Roses

During the fifteenth century the Crown was drawn into the struggles between great men. Groups of nobles tried to get their supporters on the council and to gain the favour of the king. If they failed, they sometimes supported someone else who had a claim to the throne. The Earl of Warwick earned the title 'the Kingmaker', by helping one side and then the other in the fight between the Houses of Lancaster and York, which you can see outlined in the chart on page 135.

Because the red rose was the badge of Lancaster and the white rose the badge of York, the brutal contest between them became known as the Wars of the Roses. It did not end until Henry Tudor defeated the Yorkist side and was crowned king in 1485.

So the demands for higher wages to be paid in money after the Black Death not only helped to cause Tyler's revolt, but also made it easier for great lords to hire men to fight for them in the battles between Lancaster and York. A new family of rulers, the Tudors, had to face the problems which came with the changes in the life of their people.

Richard II. This painting now hangs in Westminster Abbey.

Dates to remember

1348   The Black Death arrived in England
1381   The Peasants' Revolt

Things to do

1   In 1381 a horse could be bought for £2, an ox for 10s., a cow for 5s., a ewe with lamb for 14d., and a pig for 1s. Compare these prices with those at the time of the Black Death. How many times greater are they?
2   Find out all you can about William Langland, John Wycliffe, and John of Gaunt.
3   Imagine that you are an aged villein of fifty living in 1381. Write your life story, including the changes which you saw after the coming of the Black Death.
4   Copy the plan of London at the time of the Peasants' Revolt and underline the names of all the places visited by the rebels.

Books to read

D. M. Stuart, *The Young Londoner through the Ages*, Harrap
M. Reeves, *The Medieval Village*, Longmans

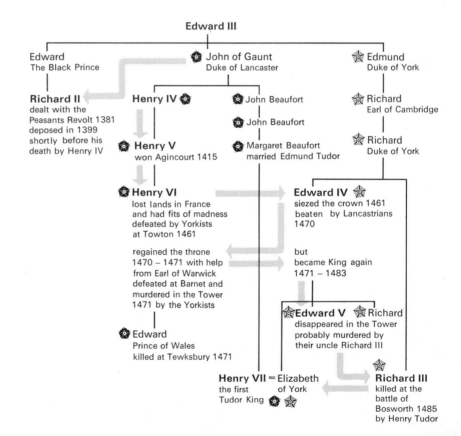

Lancaster against York.

Chapter 14
Wolsey and Cromwell – servants of a new monarchy

Both Wolsey and Cromwell were men of quite humble birth who rose to high position. Both used their great abilities ruthlessly to advance their careers and to increase the power of the king they served. When he tired of them, no one lifted a finger to save them.

How Henry VII used the middle classes

The Tudor kings who ruled England and Wales from 1485 employed such men as Wolsey and Cromwell because they owed everything to their masters. They could be dismissed at will, whereas it was often very difficult to get rid of councillors who came from the nobility. As we have seen, the Wars of the Roses were caused not only by Henry VI's madness and England's failure in the war with France, but also by a struggle for power in the council among the leading men of the kingdom.

When the crown was picked out of a thorn bush on the battlefield at Bosworth and put on Henry Tudor's head, the king had really won the contest for power with his barons which had been going on throughout the Middle Ages. Many of the old noble families had died out during the war. Those that were left had lost hold of the services of their villeins and were too poor to be much of a threat.

Henry VII made peace with the House of York by marrying Elizabeth, daughter of Edward IV, but he was clever enough to see that his best allies would be the wealthy merchants and landowners (gentry) of the middle class. He made some show of getting parliament, where their representatives sat in the House of Commons, to confirm his right to the crown. They welcomed his plan of punishing disorder because peace was good for trade. Again he pleased them by recovering royal lands which had been taken over by others and running them so efficiently that he had less need to demand taxes. He kept down expenses by avoiding wars. His one attack on France ended when he was well paid to go away. In spite of this, the other countries of Europe sought his friendship and he married two of his children into the royal houses of Spain and Scotland. Henry also made trade agreements with such countries as Flanders and Denmark, while at the same time protecting home industries from foreign competition. He even

Henry VII in 1505 holding in his hand the red rose of Lancaster.

invested his own money in the trading enterprises of his subjects and made handsome profits as a result.

Wolsey's rise to power

Thomas Wolsey became Henry's chaplain in 1507, two years before the king's death. He was the son of a butcher and cattle dealer of Ipswich. After graduating from Oxford, he entered the service of the Archbishop of Canterbury and later proved his usefulness to Fox, the Bishop of Winchester and one of the king's most able servants. The young Henry VIII dismissed most of his father's men, for they had become unpopular, but he soon saw that Wolsey's talents were too valuable to lose and made him Lord Chancellor. Later he became Archbishop of York and was made a cardinal by the Pope.

Thomas Wolsey wearing his
cardinal's hat and robes.

One foreign visitor to England described Wolsey as a handsome, eloquent and hard-working man, who gloried in his power:

This Cardinal is the person who rules the King and the whole kingdom. When the ambassador first arrived in England, he used to say to him, 'His Majesty will do so and so,' but then he slowly began to forget himself and began to say, 'We shall do so and so.' Now he has got to the point of saying, 'I shall do so and so.'

The king's justice

Part of Wolsey's work was to act as judge in two courts which the Tudor kings used to put down the 'over-mighty subject'. In the Star Chamber, a room with gold stars painted on a blue ceiling, he and other members of the council punished those who offended against the new Livery and Maintenance Act. This act was passed to stop lords from keeping more than a certain number of men who served them and wore their coats of arms. During the Wars of the Roses these men had been used as private armies to bully neighbours and to protect their lords against their enemies. Under Wolsey those who tried to do this were imprisoned or heavily fined, which was one way the king could make money. In the Court of Requests he gave justice to the poor who could not afford it elsewhere or who found themselves opposed by a rich man who could bribe juries in other courts.

A fatal mistake

Another part of Wolsey's work was to manage Henry's policy abroad, for the young king left it mainly to him. His idea was that England should take advantage of the struggle between France and the Emperor Charles V, the ruler of Spain, the Netherlands and Germany. Wolsey was anxious that England should be on the winning side. This would mean rich rewards for his master. At the same time he hoped that he himself might become Pope.

In the end Wolsey made a mistake, for in 1529 the two sides made peace – much to his surprise. Charles had already invaded Rome and gained control of the Pope. This was very serious for Wolsey, because by this time Henry was tired of his first wife, Catherine of Aragon, who had a daughter, Mary, but not the son whom Henry hoped for. Instead he wished to marry the bewitching Anne Boleyn. Only the Pope could grant a divorce and this he refused to do for fear of Charles. Catherine happened to be the emperor's aunt. Wolsey was blamed for this state of affairs.

The cardinal's fall

At the height of his power Wolsey had dressed in the finest silks, velvets and furs. He ordered a magnificent palace to be built at Hampton Court to house his fine furniture, tapestries, and a collection of silver and gold plate which was worth thousands of pounds. When he appeared in public, he had his cardinal's hat carried before him by a nobleman while he followed behind sniffing at a hollow orange. It was filled with a sponge soaked in vinegar and herbs to protect him from any disease which might be carried by the crowds who pressed around him.

So great was his pride that many must have been glad at the news that he died on his way to face a charge of treason. His

Above: Catherine of Aragon, Henry VIII's first wife; *below:* her rival, Anne Boleyn, who became Henry's second wife and queen in 1533.

Hampton Court: Queen Anne Boleyn's gateway, so called because it was redecorated for her. But it was originally built by Wolsey in 1514; his arms are over the archway. The clock, made in 1540 for Henry VIII, shows not only the time of day but the phases of the moon and the time of high water at London Bridge.

Wolsey's room at Hampton Court.

only companion has left us a vivid picture of the old man lying in the flickering candlelight and demanding that the cook be roused at four in the morning to make him some chicken broth. As it grew light, he began to think of Henry's wish for a divorce and his own fall from favour, saying,

If I had served God as diligently as I have done the King, he would not have given me over in my grey hairs. . . . He is sure a prince of royal courage and hath a princely heart; . . . I assure you I have often kneeled before him in his private chamber on my knees, the space of an hour or two to persuade him from his will and desire, but I could never bring to pass to dissuade him from it. . . . I warn you to be well advised and assured what matter ye put into his head, for ye shall never put it out again. . . .

Soon afterwards Wolsey lost the power of speech and at eight o'clock he died.

A 'knave' in power

When the great cardinal was in disgrace, no one defended him more bravely than his servant, Thomas Cromwell. At the same time his conscience did not stop him from helping to share out Wolsey's lands and money. He then attracted the notice of the king who became his new master. Henry admired Cromwell's great ability to get things done, though he despised his character. Every time he was dealt a knave at cards, he would exclaim, 'I have got Cromwell.'

Cromwell was the son of a drunken, dishonest trader. At the age of eighteen he left home to travel in Italy and the Netherlands. He returned with a good knowledge of business and banking. For a time he earned a living as a lawyer and money-lender, but his desire for power led him at last to become secretary first to Wolsey and then to the king.

Cromwell had no friends and always hid his true feelings, though he was charming to those who could be of use to him. He enjoyed making money, and was generous to others, especially to faithful servants. He would stop at nothing to increase his own and the king's power. Those who stood in his way often found themselves condemned to die on some trumped-up charge while Master Cromwell stood coldly by, secretly gloating over their fate.

Cromwell at work

We know a good deal about the way Cromwell's mind worked, for he used to jot down things he wanted to remember on loose

Thomas Cromwell.

sheets of paper. These 'remembrances', as he called them, show that he was a man of great energy. He knew everything about the army and navy. He took charge of foreign policy and tried to encourage trade. He managed elections so that there was little opposition to his plans in Parliament. He made the departments of the royal household more efficient so that it began to look something like the modern Civil Service. He even found time to design a new sort of rigging for ships and a piece of jewellery for the king.

Most important of all, he encouraged Henry in his quarrel with the Pope. He suggested that if the king were head of the Church in England, he could easily get a divorce and marry Anne Boleyn whom he loved. It would be good for the country if he could have a son to succeed him on the throne instead of his daughter, Mary, the only child of his first marriage. Also the lands and money which had belonged to the Church would make him one of the richest princes in Europe. Henry was delighted with these ideas and gave orders to carry them out.

The state of the monasteries

Some of the best lands in England belonged to the monasteries, and Cromwell soon began to collect evidence against the monks so that the king would have an excuse to be rid of them. This was not too difficult because fewer men and women were now willing to spend their lives in prayer away from the world. Even those who did become monks and nuns sometimes enjoyed better food and an easier life than St Benedict had intended. Also, many monasteries were in debt. Monks made poor businessmen and tended to be too soft-hearted to make large profits by turning their land over to sheep-farming, for less labourers would be needed and many would be turned off the land and left homeless (see pages 180–81).

Even so, many monasteries were so well run and had such a good reputation that Cromwell was often forced to use under-hand methods to get evidence against them. Those he sent out to investigate charges against the monks wrote in their letters to him that they were seeking out all the evil they could find. When they visited monasteries where even they could see nothing wrong, they sent humble letters of apology and excuse because they had displeased their master.

Usually they made their visit as much of a surprise as possible and attempted to bully the monks from the start. One of Cromwell's men behaved so badly that another wrote of him,

First in his going he is too insolent. . . . Then he handleth the fathers where he cometh very roughly, and many times for small causes, as . . . for not meeting him at the door, when they had no warning of his coming.

The visitors would question all the monks and their servants, especially those who had grudges against the abbot or the other monks and might speak against them. Then they left with 'gifts' which the monks were too frightened to refuse them.

The reports of Cromwell's men showed that some monasteries were in a bad state. At Wigmore, for instance, the abbot was said to be a murderer as well as a thief, and to be so lax that his chaplain was allowed to:

A monk in charge of the wine-cellar. Such medieval paintings helped to discredit monasteries, making it easier for Henry VIII to destroy them.

143

carry cross-bows, and to go fishing and hunting in the king's forests, parks and chases, but to do little or nothing serving the choir as other brethren do.

At Waverley the abbot was honest, but completely unable to control the other monks or his servants. Dr Layton, who visited him, complained bitterly,

Yesterday, early in the morning, sitting in my chamber in examination, I could neither get bread, drink, nor fire of these knaves till I was perished with cold and the abbot dared not speak to them.

Some of the charges against the monks seem unlikely to be true, but Henry was in no mood to disbelieve them. In 1536 the smaller monasteries were closed and the monks pensioned off and thrown out into the world.

The Pilgrimage of Grace   1536

It was in the north that the monasteries were most missed. A series of bad harvests made the people demand a return of the monks who had given food and money to the poor and taught their children. They set out on a peaceful protest march to

Right: Fountains Abbey, Yorkshire. This great Cistercian monastery was ruined when it was dissolved and its abbot executed in 1539.

A judge rides out of Colchester after the trial of Abbot Thomas Beche for his part in the Pilgrimage of Grace. His execution can be seen in the distance.

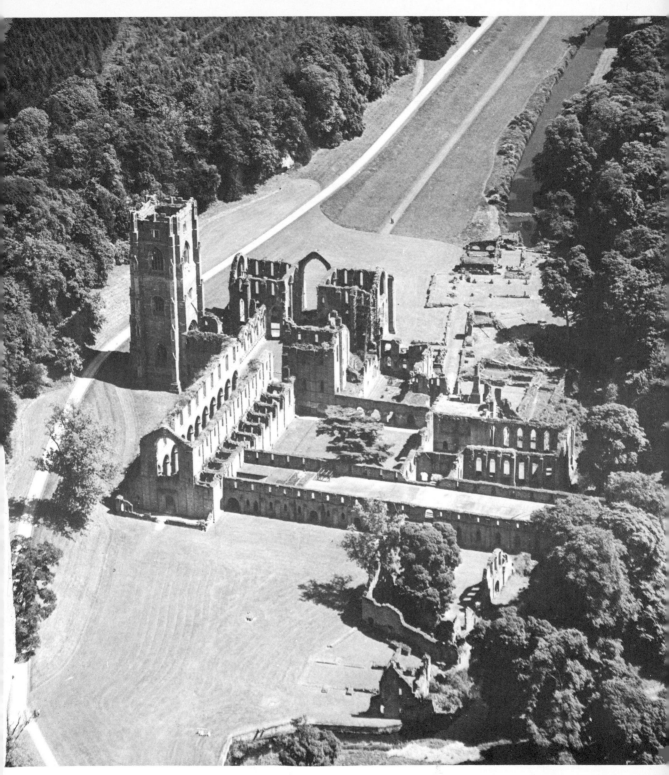

London. There they hoped to see the king and beg him to get rid of his evil advisers, including Cromwell, and to call a free Parliament which would restore the monasteries and the religion which England had known before Henry's quarrel with the Pope.

For a time the Pilgrimage of Grace, as the rising was called, seemed a danger to the government, but the Duke of Norfolk met the rebels by the River Don and in the king's name promised them a free pardon and a remedy for their complaints. He invited Robert Aske, their leader, to London for talks. By the time it was clear that Henry was not going to keep his word, most of them had gone home. Over 200 of them were executed. Robert Aske's reputation as a lawyer and local squire did not save him from being hanged from a church tower in chains until he starved to death.

Cromwell then went on to dissolve the larger monasteries. The buildings were pulled down and the stone and lead sold. Their treasures of gold and silver were taken away and sold or melted down to increase the wealth of the king. Even the manuscripts copied so carefully by the monks were sold and some of them ended up as wrapping paper in shops. Most of the land which had belonged to the monks was bought by the gentry and merchants who were eager to invest their money in land. In this way Cromwell not only made a profit for the king, but made sure that these powerful men would never want to see a return of the monks whose lands they now owned.

Cromwell's execution

Cromwell was rewarded for his part in destroying the monasteries by being made Earl of Essex. Yet in the same year Henry began to turn against him. He was angry that threats from abroad had forced him to marry the ugly princess, Anne of Cleves, so that England would have an ally in Germany. Henry blamed Cromwell for this and began to listen to his enemies. In the end he had him arrested and sentenced to die under the very laws which Cromwell had suggested in order to make it easier to condemn traitors. The king received a last appeal for 'Mercy, mercy, mercy!' from his former secretary, but he ignored it. Cromwell went to his death, protesting his loyalty, with no show of fear.

Wolsey's work for justice and Cromwell's work in destroying the monasteries lasted long after their deaths. They made the Tudor kings richer and more powerful than any of the kings of the Middle Ages. It was not until their allies in the middle class began to turn against them that serious opposition began to grow.

Anne of Cleves, painted by the court artist Hans Holbein, in about 1539. Henry was persuaded by Holbein's portraits that Anne was good-looking. When he saw her, he got a shock.

146

Dates to remember

1515   Wolsey became Lord Chancellor
1535   Visitation of the monasteries began
1540   Cromwell was executed

Things to do

1   Read through Wolsey's dying words. What do they tell you about Henry VIII's character? What was the idea that Wolsey could not get out of the king's head?
2   From what you have read about the behaviour of the men sent by Cromwell to visit the monasteries, write an account of such a visit first as if you were a monk, and then as if you were a visitor.
3   Here are some figures worked out by Henry's treasurer in the ten years after the destruction of the monasteries.

   Received:
   Revenue from monastery lands   £415,005
   Sale of monastery lands   £855,711
   Sale of buildings, bell, lead, etc.   £26,502
   Sale of silver and gold plate   £79,081
   Paid out:
   Pensions to monks and nuns   £33,045

   How much money did the king make from the monasteries?

Book to read

E. Vale, *Abbeys and Priories*, Batsford

Chapter 15
Henry VIII – a Renaissance prince

Henry VIII lived at a time of great change in Europe. The old noble families were weakened as the middle classes began to grow wealthy from trade. The Church lost some of its power after a long dispute over who should be Pope. In many of the states of Europe there ruled new families who, like the Tudors, had put an end to disorder and wished to take all power into their own hands. Most important of all, there was a rebirth or renaissance of interest in learning and the arts.

The Renaissance of Greek and Latin learning

During the Middle Ages most educated men wrote in Latin and many of the works of the Romans and Greeks were studied, though the Church did not encourage those pagan ideas which could not be made to agree with Christianity. Towards the end of the Middle Ages more writing was done in the everyday language of the people, but there was a new desire to read and discuss the writings of ancient times. This was partly caused by the arrival in Western Europe of Greek scholars fleeing from the Turks who had at last taken Constantinople. Schools where the ideas of Plato and Aristotle were studied sprang up in Italy, the Netherlands, France and Germany. The Church no longer disapproved of this. Indeed some of the renaissance popes were fine Greek scholars. Most important of all, the invention of the printing press, which was first used by Gutenberg in Germany and later by William Caxton in England, meant that books could be produced more cheaply and in greater numbers. So new ideas spread more rapidly in print.

William Caxton's device by which all the books he printed between 1487 and 1489 can be recognised. His trade-mark in the centre has his initials on either side.

A time of discovery

At the same time men were taking more interest in the world around them. Larger ships and better compasses and other aids to navigation led to longer voyages of exploration overseas. In 1492 Columbus reached the American continent after a voyage lasting over six weeks during which his crew nearly mutinied because they feared they might never see land again. In 1519 Magellan led an expedition which was to sail round the world for the first time.

Henry VIII by Holbein. Henry liked to be admired for his good figure.

In science too, men began to think and experiment for themselves instead of just accepting what they had been told. The Polish astronomer Copernicus had the astonishing idea that the sun and not the earth is the centre of the universe. So people had to face not only the surprise of finding a vast new continent on earth, but the shock of discovering that their world had a very humble place in the heavens. In spite of opposition from the Church, doctors began to cut up dead bodies to see exactly how they worked. In this way Michael Servetus, a Spaniard, found out how the blood circulated through the body by way of the heart and lungs over a hundred years before the Englishman, William Harvey, who wrote about it in detail.

Interest in the human body is also seen in renaissance painting. Artists tried to portray their subjects more realistically than the

God creating man. Part of the
ceiling of the Sistine Chapel,
Rome, painted by
Michelangelo.

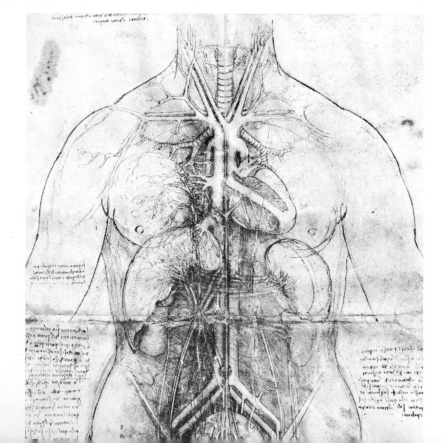

Leonardo da Vinci's drawing
of the human body. Other
artists studied anatomy to
make their paintings realistic,
but Leonardo went further and
used his skill as an artist to
show how the human body
worked.

painters of the Middle Ages. Compare Michelangelo's painting with those in earlier chapters. By the use of perspective and new types of paint they brought the people and scenes they painted alive. Others experimented in the arts of building, glass-blowing and working gold and silver.

A man of the Renaissance

The fashionable man of the Renaissance was always willing to listen to new ideas. He studied not only books but the world around him. He was expected to have a wide variety of talents, like Leonardo da Vinci, who painted such masterpieces as the Mona Lisa, as well as studying the human body and inventing early tanks and aeroplanes. Even those who had little talent themselves were expected to enjoy music, painting and poetry and to use their money to support scholars and artists of various kinds. The Medici family in Florence and the popes in Rome were especially generous. Michelangelo, for instance, painted the ceiling of the Sistine Chapel at the request of Pope Julius II, who also began plans to rebuild St Peter's. Above all, a true man of the Renaissance had the desire for fame which would last after his death.

Henry VIII as a scholar

Let us see how Henry VIII fits in with this picture of the ideal renaissance man. When he was a boy, the great scholar, Erasmus, visited his nursery and was impressed by his education. Earlier in the Middle Ages children had spent much of their time learning off by heart passages in Latin which they hardly understood. Now efforts were made to make lessons more enjoyable. One teacher, Colet, the founder of St Paul's School in London, even wrote a Latin grammar book in which the words were illustrated by pictures to help the pupils. Children were also encouraged to take part in sports which would make them healthy instead of sitting over their books all day. Henry learnt not only Latin, but Spanish, Italian, and French as well. He was taught to play the lute and read music on sight. Out of doors he rode and tilted well and was a good archer and tennis-player.

Later he made a friend of the scholar Thomas More, who was also his chancellor. Henry was often to be seen walking with More in the garden of his home at Chelsea. After dinner the two men would talk or listen to music or climb on to the roof to study the stars. More was the friend of Colet and Erasmus, who had made a translation of the New Testament from the original Greek

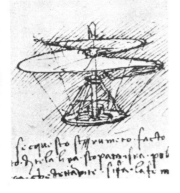

Leonardo's flying machine. He made detailed observations of bats and birds to see how they flew, but his own machine lacked the power to take off. (Leonardo wrote all his notes from right to left with the letters reversed.)

Thomas More, wearing his chancellor's chain.

Left: a woodcut of Utopia, More's imaginary island.

into Latin. Erasmus had also written a book showing the follies of mankind. Even the Church was not safe from his attack. More himself wrote a book called *Utopia*, in which he invented an imaginary country to show his ideas for the improvement of government and the customs of the people. No doubt More discussed his ideas with the king and told him about those of his friends. Henry was always pleased to receive copies of new works from their authors, although he was often too lazy to read them. He had himself written a book defending the Pope against the attacks of the German, Luther. He was rewarded with the title of 'Defender of the Faith', although someone else probably did most of the work for him.

Henry and the arts

One of the king's teachers was a poet, John Skelton, and Henry learnt to write poetry for himself. Here are two verses from one of his poems which may have been written for one of his six wives, whose fates are shown in the chart on page 167:

> As the holly groweth green,
> And never changeth hue,
> So I am, ever hath been
> Unto my lady true;
> As the holly groweth green
> With ivy all alone,
> When flowers cannot be seen
> And green leaves be gone.

Among those whom Henry employed were Thomas Tallis, the composer, and the artist Holbein, who painted portraits of the royal family and some of the leading men at court. Other artists, mostly from Italy, were set to work on the palace at Hampton Court, which Wolsey gave to the king shortly before he fell from favour.

A Machiavellian prince

Henry was not only a Renaissance man but a Renaissance prince. Earlier, in the Middle Ages, rulers had often acted cruelly and dishonestly, but they usually tried to live by the laws of God and the Church. One of the greatest kings of the time was St Louis of France. Other rulers sought his advice and judgement, not so much because he was powerful, but because he led such a holy life.

Henry VIII displaying his talents. He was famous for his lute and harp playing, and liked to appear well-read.

The ruler of the Renaissance tended to be very different. Machiavelli, an Italian, wrote *The Prince*, a book which pretended to give advice to the princes of the time. In it he took it for granted that a ruler would have to cheat, lie, and kill to keep power. It was better to be feared than to be loved. Men were ungrateful and would rebel unless they knew that a cruel punishment awaited them. A prince should appear to be generous, but he need not be so really.

Henry would never have agreed that Machiavelli's advice was right; on the other hand he acted as though it was. Several times he killed because it suited him. He hardly pretended to give his victims a fair trial. Empson and Dudley, two lawyers who had served his father well, were executed because the heavy fines they collected made them unpopular. By their deaths Henry hoped to make his people think well of him. Anne Boleyn, his second wife, was condemned to die because the king was tired of her and because she had no son. Even his former friend, More, was sentenced to death because he could not agree that Henry and not the Pope was head of the Church in England. He offered to give up his post as chancellor and to keep quiet about his views, but nothing less than absolute obedience would satisfy the king. More was a man loved and respected by nearly all who knew him and his example might be followed by others. In spite of the threat of death and the nagging of his wife, Dame Alice, who did not understand why he was being so obstinate, More would not act against his conscience.

Shortly before he died he wrote a letter to his daughter, Margaret:

Mine own good daughter. Our Lord be thanked I am in good health of body and in good quiet mind. I beseech Him make you merry in the hope of heaven. . . . Who bless and preserve you all. Written with a coal by your tender loving father, who in his poor prayers forgetteth none of you all. . . . And thus fare you heartily well for lack of paper.

To the last More remained cheerful and even joked with the man who helped him on to the scaffold,

See me safe up, and for my coming down, let me shift (manage) for myself.

Henry was probably no worse than other rulers of his time. He made his power so absolute that no man could defy him with safety and so there was peace. All Europe admired his talents as

The Great Hall, Hampton Court, built by Henry VIII in 1531 to replace Wolsey's smaller hall. The king and his guests sat on a platform at the far end of the hall, before an open hearth. The smoke found its way out through an opening in the roof.

scholar, poet, musician and sportsman. In spite of the fate that awaited them, women were eager to marry him and men to serve him. He was a true prince of the Renaissance.

Dates to remember

1492 Columbus sailed to America
1530 Copernicus put forward his new theory about the universe
1533 Michelangelo was at work in the Sistine Chapel.

Things to do

1 What sign can you see on a modern coin that Henry was ever given the title *Fidei Defensor* (Defender of the Faith), by the Pope? Why is it strange that rulers of England still use it to this day?

2 Read More's last letter carefully. What sort of man does it show that he was? Do you get the same impression by looking at his portrait? How was the king being especially mean to More while he was in prison?

3 Here are two points from Machiavelli's advice. Can you think of any examples of Henry VIII acting in the same way?

(a) A prince ought to help able men and honour those who are gifted in the Arts. . . . Also he ought to entertain the people with festivals and shows.
(b) A prince who keeps his subjects loyal ought not to mind being thought cruel, because in the end he will be kinder than those rulers who are too kind and allow disorders to arise.

4 Here is a list of some of Henry's expenses. How did he spend most of his money? What sort of things would his household expenses include?

Wages	£14,444	3s.	4½d.
Purchase of lands	£51,749	9s.	9½d.
Presents of gold and silverplate	£14,619	12s.	10¼d.
War expenses	£546,530	0s.	8¾d.
Ships and defences for the coast	£92,407	7s.	9 d.
Household expenses	£274,086	19s.	8¾d.

5 Find out what you can about these men of the Renaissance: Copernicus, Caxton, Leonardo da Vinci, Michelangelo, Erasmus, More, Skelton, Colet, and Tallis.

Armour made for Henry VIII at his workshops in Greenwich. It can be seen today in the Tower of London.

156

Books to read
M. Stanley-Wrench, *The Story of Sir Thomas More*, Methuen
Barbara Leonie Picard, *The Tower and the Traitors*, Batsford
Eric Allen, *The Story of Lorenzo the Magnificent*, Faber
J. Thomas, *Leonardo da Vinci*, Muller

Henry VIII jousting before
Catherine of Aragon and her
ladies in 1510. This
entertainment was held to
mark the birth of a son to
Catherine, but the baby died
soon after.

Chapter 16
Archbishop Cranmer and the Reformation in England

The gentle archbishop

Thomas Cranmer remained safe for so long in time of danger because he appeared weak and defenceless. In the reign of Henry VIII he lived on while other more forceful characters ended on the block. Only when faced with death for his beliefs did his courage and strength of character show to the full.

King Henry felt a certain affection for the gentle scholar whom he had made Archbishop of Canterbury. He once told Cranmer of a plot to accuse him of treason and arranged a little scene in which he brought the archbishop face to face with his accusers, and then sided with him. No one dared attack him after that. When Queen Catherine Howard was to be beheaded for being unfaithful to the king, only Cranmer dared plead for her life. Since she and her friends favoured the Catholic side and had done their best to get rid of him, his action was both brave and unselfish at a time when most people were eager to save only themselves. In the king's last hours he was comforted in his fear of death by the archbishop who sat by him, holding his hand.

Cranmer and Luther

Cranmer had studied the Scriptures at Cambridge and was sent abroad to get the support of other learned men in Germany for Henry's divorce from his first wife. There he came to know more of the ideas of Martin Luther. Luther was the son of a miner. He was an able scholar and became a monk so that he could continue his studies in peace. Much about the Church worried him, especially when he visited Rome and saw how the popes of the Renaissance seemed to care more for worldly learning, art and pleasure than for God.

Later when Luther was teaching in the university of Wittenburg, Tetzel, a messenger from the Pope, came round selling indulgences in aid of the fund to rebuild St Peter's church in Rome. He told people that their own sins and those of anyone they loved would be forgiven if they gave generously, claiming, 'As the coin in the box doth ring, the soul from purgatory forth can spring.'

Luther preaching.

In this engraving, made by a follower of Luther in 1525, forgiveness from Christ (bottom right) outweighs indulgences from the Pope (top left).

Luther nailed ninety-five reasons why Tetzel was wrong on the door of the local church and soon found himself accused of heresy. At the end of his trial before the Emperor Charles V at Worms he still refused to change his views, saying, 'Here I stand, I can do no other.' For this he was outlawed, but the German princes kidnapped him for his own safety. They used his ideas as an excuse

The Pope as Supreme Head of the Church receives the homage of the princes of the world who kneel before him. The artist was a Protestant and disapproved of papal power.

to break with the Pope and take over the lands and wealth of the Church. The invention of printing meant that Luther's views soon became widely known throughout Europe.

Cranmer agreed with Luther on several points. Both men believed that a Christian was saved by his faith in God and in His son, Jesus. Giving money to the Church had little to do with it. As Luther said, 'Those who say that the soul flies out of purgatory (to heaven) as the coin tinkles in the box are preaching an idea thought up by man.' Cranmer also followed Luther in holding that the Pope of Rome had no more authority than any other bishop and that the teaching of the Church should only be accepted when it agreed with what was to be found in the Bible. This should be translated into the language of the people so that anyone could read it, and not just the clergy who knew Latin.

Worst of all to those who remained true to the Church, neither Luther nor Cranmer believed that at the Mass the bread and wine did really turn into the body and blood of Christ.

Why the Church was unpopular

Others besides Cranmer were eager to change the Church in England. The Church courts were hated for the way they punished people for their sins. A tailor, Richard Hunne, was found hanged in prison while awaiting trial for heresy. His real crime was that he had refused to pay a fee to a priest for the burial of his child. His jailers were suspected of murdering him in an effort to silence his protests. They escaped with their lives because clergymen could not be tried in the king's courts.

Many priests seemed unworthy to serve God. Some great churchmen were guilty of pluralism – that is, they held many offices in the Church at the same time. Wolsey was Archbishop of York, Abbot of St Albans and Bishop of Bath and Wells. He could not do all these jobs and serve the king as well, so he kept the money they brought in and paid lesser men to do the work for him. Many of the clergy were also ignorant and worldly. Some of them barely knew what the Latin words of Church services meant. Others, like Cranmer, had wives, though forbidden to marry.

In many ways the Church was not much worse than it had ever been, but the men of the Renaissance looked at it with a new, critical spirit and noticed its bad points. Some of them, like the king, set greedy eyes on its lands and wealth.

Henry's break with Rome

The king's quarrel with the Pope over the royal divorce gave those who wished to reform the Church their chance. Cranmer was made archbishop and soon gave his opinion that Henry's marriage to his first wife was unlawful because she had first been betrothed to his elder brother, Arthur, who had died.

Already Henry was determined to be master in his own kingdom. He got parliament to declare that 'The king our sovereign lord . . . shall be taken, accepted and reputed the only supreme head in earth of the Church of England.' The king now had control of all Church courts and property. Pluralities were forbidden. The clergy could be tried for their crimes in the king's courts. As you have read, the monasteries were destroyed.

Yet in Henry VIII's time few other changes were made. The king kept the services of the Church much as he had always known them. Only the creed and the Lord's prayer were translated into

Thomas Cranmer, 1546. His dress is simpler than that of archbishops before the Reformation.

English along with the Bible. Otherwise the old Latin prayer book, the Missal, was used.

The Reformation in Edward VI's reign

Since the king was now head of the Church in England, a change of ruler often led to changes in religion. As you can see from the family tree on page 167, the boy-king Edward, the son of Henry VIII and his third wife, Jane Seymour, came to the throne on his father's death. The real power in the country was in the hands first of the Duke of Somerset, who would have liked to pursue a policy of tolerance over religious matters, and later the Duke of Northumberland, who overthrew Somerset and appeared friendly to the Protestant side, though his chief concern was to keep power for himself. They encouraged Cranmer to make reforms in the worship of the Church. Others who had seen the work of the reformers Calvin and Zwingli in Switzerland were also anxious for changes to be made. For the first time Protestant ideas were widely talked about and accepted in England.

Cranmer produced an English Prayer Book which is like the one in use today. In it he altered the communion service so that those who agreed with Luther and those who did not were both

Henry VIII on his death-bed in 1547. His son, Edward VI, sits enthroned. On his left are Edward, Duke of Somerset, John, Duke of Northumberland, and Cranmer, Archbishop of Canterbury.

Queen Mary Tudor in 1553.

able to accept it. Worship and the churches themselves became plainer. Statues, pictures, candles and gorgeous robes tended to disappear, because it was thought that they took the worshippers' attention away from the service. The shrines of saints were destroyed and the beautiful and costly things which had been offered there went to the Crown. Guilds which had been formed to pray for the dead were also abolished as being useless. Some of the money from them went to found new schools. Cranmer may not have liked the way in which some of the grasping men at court made a profit out of these changes. He did not protest because he firmly believed that the king had the right to govern the Church as he wished.

The return of the Roman Catholic faith

In the next reign Cranmer's belief was put to the test. Edward wilted under the strain of too much study and work on state papers. At the age of sixteen he died of consumption. For a time the Protestant party tried to put Lady Jane Grey, the Duke of Northumberland's daughter-in-law, on the throne. She was only queen for nine days before the forces of Mary Tudor, Henry VIII's elder daughter, took control. Lady Jane Grey, who had scarcely known a moment's happiness in her young life, was executed. Before she died she was made to look upon the headless body of her husband.

The new queen was a Catholic. As a girl she had remained true to her faith even when she saw Thomas More and others dying for their loyalty to the Pope. She at once set out to undo much of Cranmer's work. The Pope was once more head of the Church in England. The Church courts were brought back. Even Mary, however, could not force the middle-class members of parliament to vote for a return of the monasteries. It was those people who had gained lands or wealth from the Church who were now most firmly Protestant and determined to oppose the queen.

Cranmer did not know whether to defy Mary or to keep his rule of obedience to the Crown. At last the queen, who was advised by her husband, Philip of Spain, and her bishops, began to put Protestant heretics on trial. Most of those found guilty and burned were humble people. Still the queen wished Cranmer to submit as an example to others. He was put on trial at Oxford. After hours of questioning and argument he was persuaded to admit that his Protestant beliefs were wrong. He did so believing that his life would be spared.

Few who have ever read accounts of death by burning will blame him. From the window of his prison Cranmer saw two other bishops, Latimer and Ridley, going to die. Latimer comforted his friend, saying, 'We shall this day light such a candle as I trust shall never be put out.' His death was mild in comparison to Ridley's. Relatives tried to shorten Ridley's sufferings by piling on faggots, which were green and would not burn. As a result his legs were burned away while the rest of him was untouched. Only when the flames reached the bag of gunpowder which had been placed around his neck did his agony end.

Cranmer's death

Cranmer was dragged weeping through the rain to confess his faults at St Mary's church in Oxford. A special platform was set up and you can see if you go there that one of the pillars was cut away to make room for it. The congregation settled back to listen and soon received a shock. Instead of meekly confessing his faults, Cranmer bravely defended his Protestant beliefs and was sorry only for what he had written to please the queen. He said,

Forasmuch as my hand offended, writing contrary to my heart, my hand shall first be punished for it; and when I come to the fire, it shall first be burned. And as for the Pope I refuse him . . .

Martyrs at the stake in Oxford, 1555. Latimer *(left)* is saying, 'Father in heaven receive my soul' and Ridley, 'Into thy hands, O Lord', as the fire begins. Cranmer *(top right)* watches from his prison.

L. Receiue my spirit.

Frier Iohn.

Cranmer burning his right hand. The friar *(left)* had argued with the archbishop all the way to the stake in a final effort to get him to change his mind. This and the previous engraving are from Foxe's *Book of Martyrs.*

Almost at once Cranmer was hurried off to execution with cries of 'Shut the heretic's mouth.'

Foxe, in his *Book of Martyrs*, gives us this description of Cranmer's death:

His shirt was long, down to his feet which were bare; and his head, when both his caps were off was so bare that one hair could not be seen on it. His beard was long and thick. . . . The iron chain was tied round Cranmer . . . and when the wood was kindled and the fire began to burn near him, he put his right hand into the flame, which he held so steadfast and immoveable that all men might see his hand burned before his body was touched. . . . His eyes were lifted up to heaven, and oftentimes he repeated, 'This unworthy right hand,' so long as his voice would suffer him, and using often the words of Stephen, 'Lord Jesus receive my spirit,' in the greatness of the flames he gave up the ghost.

Cranmer's work did not die with him. After Mary's death the

new queen, Elizabeth I, brought Cranmer's version of the Bible and Prayer Book into use. By his courageous death he set an example of loyalty to Protestant ideas which others followed. It is Cranmer rather than Henry VIII who deserves to be remembered as the founder of the Church of England.

Dates to remember

1521   Luther's trial at Worms
1535   Henry VIII became 'Supreme Head' of the English Church
1556   Cranmer was burnt at Oxford

Things to do

1   Do you know of a school which was founded in the sixteenth century? Where did the money for it come from?

Part of the charter of the Free Grammar School at Morpeth, Northumberland, given in 1552. The king is Edward VI.

2 Have a look at a *Book of Common Prayer* and find out the sort of language which Cranmer wrote. Make a list of the services which it contains. If you can, compare them with the services which are in the Missal (the prayer book which Roman Catholics use today).

3 Read the account of Cranmer's death. What does it tell you about his looks and character?

4 Find out all you can about Luther, Calvin and Zwingli. Why do you think they are all known as 'Protestants'?

Books to read

F. C. Happold, *Everyone's Book about the English Church*, Faber
L. Diamond, *How we got our Bible*, Oxford University Press

The Tudors.

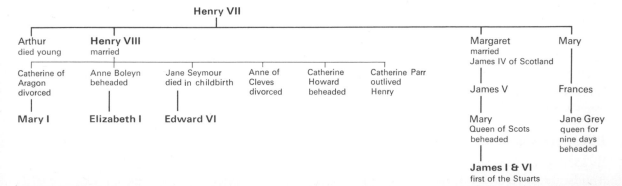

Chapter 17
Queen Elizabeth I – a woman in power

Queen Elizabeth was the first successful woman ruler in the history of England. The reigns of Matilda and Mary Tudor had brought misery and rebellion. It was not thought possible for a queen to govern without the help of a suitable husband. Yet Elizabeth managed to turn her qualities as a woman to her advantage. She played upon her charm and her seeming weakness, so that all men became suitors for her favour. Her grace and beauty hid an iron will, a fiery temper and a keen intelligence.

A princess in danger

Elizabeth learnt the value of caution early in life. Her mother, Anne Boleyn, was beheaded on the orders of her father before the little princess was three. She was so neglected that her nurse complained that she had no clothes to wear. Later Henry began to like his daughter for her quickness of wit and she was restored to favour. His last wife, Catherine Parr, took a fancy to the child and brought her up in her household.

Even in the reign of her Protestant brother, Edward, Elizabeth was suspected of a plot with the Duke of Somerset's brother, who wished to marry her. When her sister, Mary, came to the throne, she was in even greater danger. She chose to remain a Protestant, with the result that she was a natural suspect when there was a plot against the queen. She was closely questioned, but she was never trapped into admitting anything. 'Much suspected by me, nothing proved can be,' she is said to have scratched on a window-pane. In 1554 she was taken into the Tower by barge through Traitor's Gate. Only her sister's wish to show mercy saved her from the block. Never did Elizabeth show signs of anger or hurt pride. She even pretended to think of becoming a Catholic. She knew that many hated Mary for her burning of heretics and the favour she showed to the Spaniards who swarmed into England after her marriage with Philip of Spain. Elizabeth had only to wait.

Elizabeth's popularity

In 1558 after vain hopes that she was to have a child, Mary died. Amidst great rejoicing Elizabeth became queen. She was twenty-

Traitor's Gate, Tower of London. Elizabeth was taken through here in 1554, loudly protesting her innocence.

Elizabeth in 1575.

five years of age, with red-gold hair, a pleasing figure, and beautiful eyes. She had been taught by Roger Ascham, one of the best teachers of his time, who believed that learning should be a pleasure and that women should be educated as well as men. As a result Elizabeth could write Latin and Greek well. She could also speak French, Italian and Spanish, ride, sing, dance and play chess. Both her handwriting and her needlework were excellent.

Above all, Elizabeth knew the art of pleasing her subjects. She moved fearlessly through the largest crowds, noticing the poor or elderly, and praising the village which had been tidied up for her visit. She made it clear that the smallest bunch of flowers offered in loyalty delighted her. Once when a nervous schoolmaster was too frightened to speak his speech she called out, 'Be not afraid!' Afterwards she told him, 'It is the best I ever heard. Here, you shall have my hand.'

So that more of her people might see her, the queen often moved around the country, staying at the houses of the wealthy. She paid for food and other necessaries, but most of those she visited provided expensive gifts and entertainments. Once the Earl of Hertford enlarged his house and had a lake dug in the grounds when he knew she was coming. In spite of rain, Elizabeth

Elizabeth carried in procession with her courtiers in 1601. Although the queen was ageing (the artist has politely concealed this), she still realized the importance of showing herself to her subjects.

was able to enjoy a water pageant, a firework display and a banquet at which 1,000 glass and silver dishes were served by 200 servants. She left with a present of jewels.

The queen kept a magnificent court and attracted to it all the leading men of the kingdom. She had hundreds of dresses and the Scottish ambassador reported that she wore the fashion of a different country each evening. She surrounded herself with gifted men such as the musician, William Byrd, and Edmund Spenser, whose long poem, *The Faerie Queene*, was written in her honour. She paid companies of actors to perform before her. The livelier of Elizabeth's subjects spent their time enjoying the amusements at court instead of brooding on rebellion at home.

The disappointed suitors

Early in the queen's reign suitors for her hand in marriage appeared. The Spanish ambassador assured his master, 'If she decides to marry out of the country, she will at once fix her eyes on your majesty.' Only a month later, when he had seen Elizabeth's teasing ways, he admitted, 'I am afraid we shall find this woman married and I shall be the last man to know anything about it.' The princes of Austria, Sweden and France also courted her.

Elizabeth receives a book of poems by Gascoigne, published in 1575 and dedicated to her.

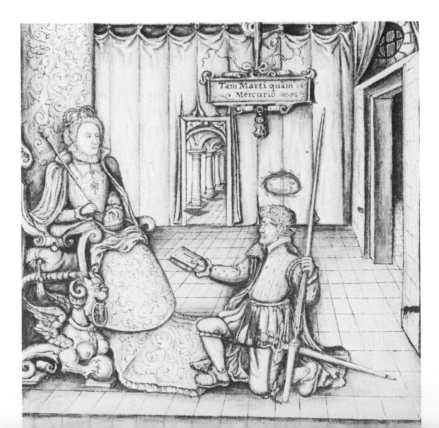

Even at the age of forty-five she raised the hopes of the French Duke of Alençon, whom she lovingly called her frog.

Of course the real reason why the Queen of England had so many suitors was that they believed her husband would be able to control the country. Elizabeth came to hate this idea. She loved only one man, the Earl of Leicester, and he was married already. Later his wife was found dead at the foot of a staircase in Cumnor Place, near Oxford. Some people believed that she was murdered, and of course her husband had the best motive. The scandal was too great for the queen to think of marrying him. She chose instead the wiser course of playing one suitor and his country off against another.

The Earl of Leicester. Elizabeth remained fond of him until he died in 1588, shortly after the defeat of the Armada.

Trouble with Spain

Soon it became clear that the real danger came from Spain. English seamen captured Spanish treasure ships on their way home from South America. They also carried slaves across from Africa and sold them to the Spanish colonists, although they were forbidden to do so. Elizabeth expressed her sincere regret to the Spanish ambassador, who knew very well that the English pirates gave her a share of their profits and that she had knighted one of their leaders, Francis Drake. England also sent help to the Protestant Dutch in revolt against the Spanish king who ruled their country.

In reply, Spain encouraged Catholics in Ireland to rebel against English rule. Once he was certain that he could not make England Catholic again by the peaceful act of marrying Elizabeth, Philip of Spain plotted to have her killed and replaced by Mary, Queen of Scots, her cousin. She was the next heir to the English throne and a staunch Catholic.

Mary, Queen of Scots

The two women were very different from each other. Mary was dark-haired and attractive, but she was not very intelligent and usually let her heart rule her head. Her first marriage to the king of France was happy, but after he died she returned to Scotland and married her handsome cousin, Lord Darnley. She came to hate him because he murdered her servant, David Rizzio, in a fit of jealousy. When Darnley was killed in a mysterious explosion, she allowed herself to be carried off and married by Lord Bothwell, one of the chief suspects for the crime. The Protestants in Scotland were led by John Knox, who shared many of Calvin's ideas. They had already been shocked by Mary's gay, pleasure-

Mary, Queen of Scots. Mary's beauty was well known.

loving ways. Now they rebelled and she was imprisoned. After a daring escape she made a desperate ride to safety in England.

Elizabeth had always been jealous of her cousin. She once gave the Scottish ambassador a very uncomfortable time as she questioned him as to whether Mary's looks and talents were better than her own. Now she was pleased that Mary's son, James, was to be brought up as a Protestant in Scotland. She hoped that he would come to the English throne on her death. Yet the problem of Mary remained. To send her back to Scotland would mean her death. Instead she was kept in prison.

On at least four occasions she was involved in attempts to kill Elizabeth and seize the throne. Finally, after the discovery of a plot led by Anthony Babington, who had been one of Mary's pages, Elizabeth hardened her heart and signed her cousin's death warrant. The execution took place at Fotheringay Castle. An eyewitness tells us that Mary appeared cheerful and

helped to make ready herself, putting on a pair of sleeves with her own hands which they (her ladies) had pulled off, and that with some haste, as if she longed to be gone. . . . Then lying upon the block most quietly, and stretching out her arms, she cried, 'Into thy hands, O Lord,' three or four times. Then, lying very still upon the block,

Execution of Mary, Queen of Scots at Fotheringay in 1587. This drawing shows Mary's entry into the hall *(top left)*, her disrobing *(centre)*, and the final blow *(top right of enclosure)*. It was made by Robert Beale who took the death warrant to Fotheringay and read it aloud to the crowd before the execution.

one of the executioners holding her slightly with one of his hands, she endured two strokes of the other executioner with an axe, she making very small noise or none at all, and not stirring any part of her from the place where she lay: and so the executioner lift up her head to the view of all the assembly and bade 'God save the Queen.' Then, her dress of lawn falling off her head, it appeared as grey as one of three score and ten years old."

Mary's pet dog lay whimpering and blood-stained near her body.

The Armada

Mary's final act of revenge was to make Philip of Spain her heir. In 1588, a year after her death, he tried to invade England and make good his claim to the throne. A great fleet called the Armada set out to collect an army from the Netherlands and carry it across the Channel. The English Admiral Howard found the Spanish ships at anchor in Calais harbour. He sent blazing ships in amongst them and they at once made for the open sea in great confusion.

The English ships were waiting for them and, helped by favourable winds, managed to destroy several enemy vessels and drive

An engraving based on the Elizabethan tapestry of the Armada. The original tapestry has not survived.

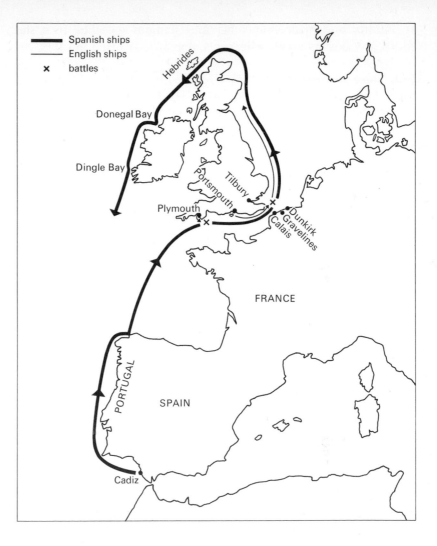

Route of the Spanish
Armada.

others on to sandbanks. The English used their powerful guns
to good effect without coming within range of the Spaniards.
The Spanish commander, Medina Sidonia, was used to an enemy
who tried to grapple one ship to another and then engaged in
hand-to-hand fighting. He was thrown into a panic by damage
caused by an enemy he could not reach. At last he decided to
brave the stormy weather and to sail into the North Sea, around
the northern tip of the British Isles and back to Spain. On the
way many galleons were wrecked and their crews drowned or
murdered by local inhabitants in search of loot. Less than half the
Armada returned home. Danger from Spain was almost at an end.

When the Spanish fleet was sighted, and beacons were lit on
the hilltops to warn of its approach, the queen reviewed her troops

at Tilbury and made one of her most famous speeches. In it she ended any doubts about whether a woman was fitted to rule:

I am come amongst you . . . being resolved in the midst of the heat of battle to live or die amongst you all, to lay down for my God, and for my kingdom, and for my people my honour and my blood, even in the dust. I know I have the body of a weak and feeble woman, but I have the heart and stomach of a king, and a King of England too.

Essex and Ireland

Englishmen could not believe the danger from Spain was almost at an end after the Armada. In the later years of Elizabeth's reign, Robert, Earl of Essex, became the leader of a group which wanted stronger action against the enemy. The queen was fond of the brilliant young man, who was Leicester's stepson, but she knew his pride, ambition and violent temper.

In 1559 Essex was put in command of an expedition to Ireland. The Irish were mostly poor and full of hatred for the English who had conquered, but could not control, their country. They remained true to the Catholic faith and looked to Spain for help in their rebellions against Elizabeth's government.

Essex's task was to crush the powerful rebel leader, the Earl of Tyrone, and so prevent a possible Spanish invasion. Instead, he met Tyrone and made peace with him. Elizabeth was furious. She feared that Essex was plotting against her and he was called back to England. For a time the queen could not bring herself to put him on trial, but he tried to make the city of London rebel in his favour. The evidence of his treason was too plain to be ignored. Essex was tried and condemned. He died with great courage, saying, 'I owe God a death.'

The Earl of Essex in 1597 when he was at the height of his power and favour with the queen.

The death of the queen

The young earl's great mistake was to believe that he could rule Elizabeth. In old age her mind was still clear and forceful. Even when she lay dying at Richmond, her will was so strong that her attendants could not force her to take food or medicine. The queen turned her face to the wall and waited silently for death. Many people of her own time and later have tried to explain the secret of Elizabeth's success. She herself was in no doubt about it, saying to her subjects, 'Though God hath raised me high, yet this I count the glory of my reign, that I have reigned with your loves.'

Dates to remember

1558   Elizabeth became queen
1587   The execution of Mary, Queen of Scots
1588   The Spanish Armada was defeated

Things to do

1   Imagine you are writing to a friend to tell how Elizabeth I came to your village. Describe the celebrations which might have taken place and the appearance and manner of the queen.

2   Here is a description of Queen Elizabeth as an old lady:

> Her face (was) oblong, fair but wrinkled; her eyes small, yet black and pleasant; her nose a little hooked; her lips narrow and her teeth black (a defect the English seem subject to for their too great use of sugar); . . . she wore false hair and that red, . . . her hands were small, her fingers long, and her stature neither tall nor low. She had a stately manner, and her way of speaking was mild and obliging. That day she was dressed in white silk, bordered with petals the size of beans, and over it a cloak of black, shot through with silver.

    In what ways had Elizabeth changed and in what ways was she still the same as she had been as a younger woman?

3   Find out all you can about Roger Ascham, Edmund Spenser, William Byrd and the Earl of Leicester.

4   Read the account of Mary, Queen of Scots' death. What sort of person does it show her to have been?

5   After the Armada, Elizabeth ordered medals bearing the words 'He blew and they were scattered,' to be made. Which do you think did most damage to the Spanish fleet, God and the weather, or the skill of the English seamen? Remember that the Spanish lost about half their fleet in this way: two captured, three lost in France, two lost in Holland, two sunk in battle, nineteen wrecked in Scotland or Ireland, fate unknown, thirty-five.

Books to read

A. Cammiade, *Elizabeth the First*, Methuen
Rosemary Sutcliff, *Houses and History*, Batsford
E. Kyle, *Queen of Scots*, Nelson

Chapter 18
Life in Elizabethan England

The queen's government

Queen Elizabeth ruled with the help of about twenty leading men who made up her Privy (secret) Council. She often spoke to them one at a time so that they should not get together and agree to give the same advice. Elizabeth liked to hear a number of different opinions and then make up her own mind. She then gave her orders to William Cecil, the secretary to the council. If a new law was needed, he arranged with the councillors who sat in parliament to get it passed. Otherwise he passed on the queen's orders directly to the Justices of the Peace. These were local men of good family who were chosen to carry out the government's wishes in the country.

Cecil was therefore important in two ways. Firstly he was the councillor who saw the queen most often. Secondly he was the link between the council, parliament, and the rest of the country. Part of Cecil's work was to make alliances with friendly powers, such as France, and to avoid war with others such as Spain. He also helped to track down traitors, especially those who supported Mary, Queen of Scots, and had a large network of spies working for him. It is not surprising that Elizabeth called Cecil her 'spirit', and showed her affection for him by feeding him with her own hands as he lay dying.

One of the biggest problems which the queen and her councillors faced was how to cut her expenses and increase her income. Elizabeth could not manage on the rents which came in from royal lands, for the cost of government was rising all the time.

William Cecil, Lord Burghley.

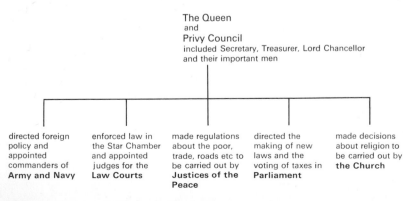

The Queen
and
Privy Council
included Secretary, Treasurer, Lord Chancellor
and their important men

directed foreign policy and appointed commanders of **Army and Navy**	enforced law in the Star Chamber and appointed judges for the **Law Courts**	made regulations about the poor, trade, roads etc to be carried out by **Justices of the Peace**	directed the making of new laws and the voting of taxes in **Parliament**	made decisions about religion to be carried out by **the Church**

Elizabeth and her
Privy Council.

She was forced to demand more taxes – to the anger of the upper classes who paid most of them. War was a disaster for her because it cost such a lot. Even her leading councillors were not well paid and increased their incomes by taking 'gifts' from those who wanted their help. Cecil left a large fortune in gold plate which he probably got in this way, and he was an honest man.

The poor

Under Elizabeth the government grew strong enough to deal with matters which affected the lives of even the humblest people. So much so that the country landowners and merchants, who had welcomed the firm rule of the Tudors, now began to resent interference which cost them money in taxes and sometimes stopped them making a profit when they had the chance. They were especially annoyed at the way the council tried to help the poor.

By now all labourers were freemen who worked for wages and paid rent for a cottage and some land. Their freedom made them

A tenant comes in to pay the rent, 1523. By the sixteenth century, rents were nearly always paid in money, not kind.

A beggar entreating help from a rich man. The woodcut is intended to attack the rich for ignoring the poor.

less secure than the villeins of the Middle Ages who had been certain of their land, which they received in return for their labour. In hard times the lord of the manor had sometimes given them extra help to prevent them from starving. Now the poor were not certain of getting work or of being able to pay the rent.

The sixteenth century was a time of rising prices. As the numbers of people grew, there was a greater demand for food. Also gold and silver came flooding into Europe from the newly discovered Spanish and Portuguese lands in South America. Since these precious metals were now more common, they were worth less. The value of a gold or silver coin fell so that less and less could be bought with it. Prices rose much faster than wages so the poor suffered most from these changes.

Even the landowners were in difficulties. Some put up rents and tried to make their land more efficient by sharing out the land in the three big open fields so that each farmer had his land all together in one place instead of in scattered strips. They still needed labourers, but since farming was a business to them, they employed as few as they could. Any man who grew old or sick knew that he would lose his job. Other landowners saw that with the growth of the woollen industry there were good profits to be

Dishonest beggars. The man on the right is off to display his wooden leg and large family to coax money from any soft-hearted passers-by. On the left, his wife drinks off the profits.

made from sheep-farming. They fenced in or enclosed their land and the commons on which the villagers had grazed their cattle. Most of their farm-workers were sacked except for one or two who were needed as shepherds. The government passed laws against enclosure for sheep-farming, but they had little effect.

In earlier times the monasteries had helped to care for the poor, but they had been destroyed in the reign of Henry VIII. This left the aged, the sick, and the unemployed and their families without help of any kind. One writer tells us that 'They lie in the streets as is commonly seen and are permitted to die like dogs or beasts without mercy.' The government tried to help. Justices of the Peace were to see that each parish collected money called the poor-rate. It was used to provide a poorhouse where honest, poor men were provided with hemp, flax, iron and other materials on which to work. Orphans were also taught a trade there and the sick cared for, though many of them were cruelly treated by heartless overseers who looked after them.

Rogues and vagabonds

The queen and her councillors also tried to deal with the dishonest poor. Mixed in with the sick and the unemployed were those who hated the very idea of work. Now that anyone could leave the village where he was born and wander round the country at will, dishonest idlers of every sort found it easy to practise their own particular brand of villainy and then move on before they were caught.

The 'courtesy man' would speak well and wear smart clothes. He would get talking to his victim and borrow money, which, of course, he never repaid. The 'ruffler' lurked in lonely places and threatened to beat up those who refused him money. The 'hooker' or 'angler' was a travelling salesman by day, but at night he fixed a hook in the top of his stick and pushed it through open windows to fish out valuables which he had spotted inside the houses he visited. Others begged for a living. The 'Abraham man' pretended he was mad, while the 'counterfeit crank' smeared himself with blood and claimed that he was ill. The 'freshwater mariner' would tell tales of his voyages with Drake or some other famous seaman to get sympathy, though he had very likely never been to sea at all.

Parliament passed stern laws against these rogues. They could be whipped and branded, and if they offended repeatedly they could be banished or hanged.

A design from an Elizabethan armourer's notebook.

Towns and trade

Like the poor and unemployed, rogues often made for the towns where they hoped to make their fortunes. Many of them must have been disappointed, for at this time trade was declining. No town except London was increasing in size and wealth.

Guilds now had less power. In their place rose the new class of merchant capitalists. They had money (capital) which they used to buy up wool and pay people to weave it. They then collected and sold the finished cloth. One of them, John Winchcombe, made a huge fortune while paying his workers only about sixpence a day.

The queen's government tried to take the place of the guilds which had fixed wages and prices in the past. The time of apprenticeship was fixed at seven years and labourers were to be hired for a year at a time. This was to make workers more secure in their jobs. Wages were to be fixed by a Justice of the Peace. Still employers got round the law and tried to force wages down. Some men were so anxious to work that they were willing to accept less than the proper wage. Merchants also left the towns and employed cottagers in their own homes so they were not so easy to control.

In an effort to bring more work to the towns, the council

Making coins in 1560, the year in which Elizabeth introduced monetary reforms. The metal is heated in a furnace, weighed, hammered into shape and stamped.

tried to help trade. They encouraged the woollen industry by enforcing rules that the lower classes were not to wear cloth of gold and silver, nor velvet nor satin, which came from abroad. All working men were to wear woollen caps. To start new industries, monopolies were given to certain businessmen, who were allowed the sole right to produce, e.g. copper, or salt or brass for a number of years. The council also made grants towards the cost of expeditions overseas which might bring the country new wealth. It also took care that coins should be worth their face value and not made of base metal, for this put up prices and discouraged trade. In 1564 exports reached a record £1,100,000. Most of this was in cloth or wool, though tin, copper, beer, coal and fish also went abroad.

London life

By the time of Elizabeth, London was famous, not only as a great and wealthy port, but also as a centre of fashion and amusement. Countrymen were despised for their dowdy clothes, their slowness of movement and wit. It became smart to visit the capital.

The newcomer to London was struck at once by the noise and bustle of city life. Carts and coaches thundered past. The sound

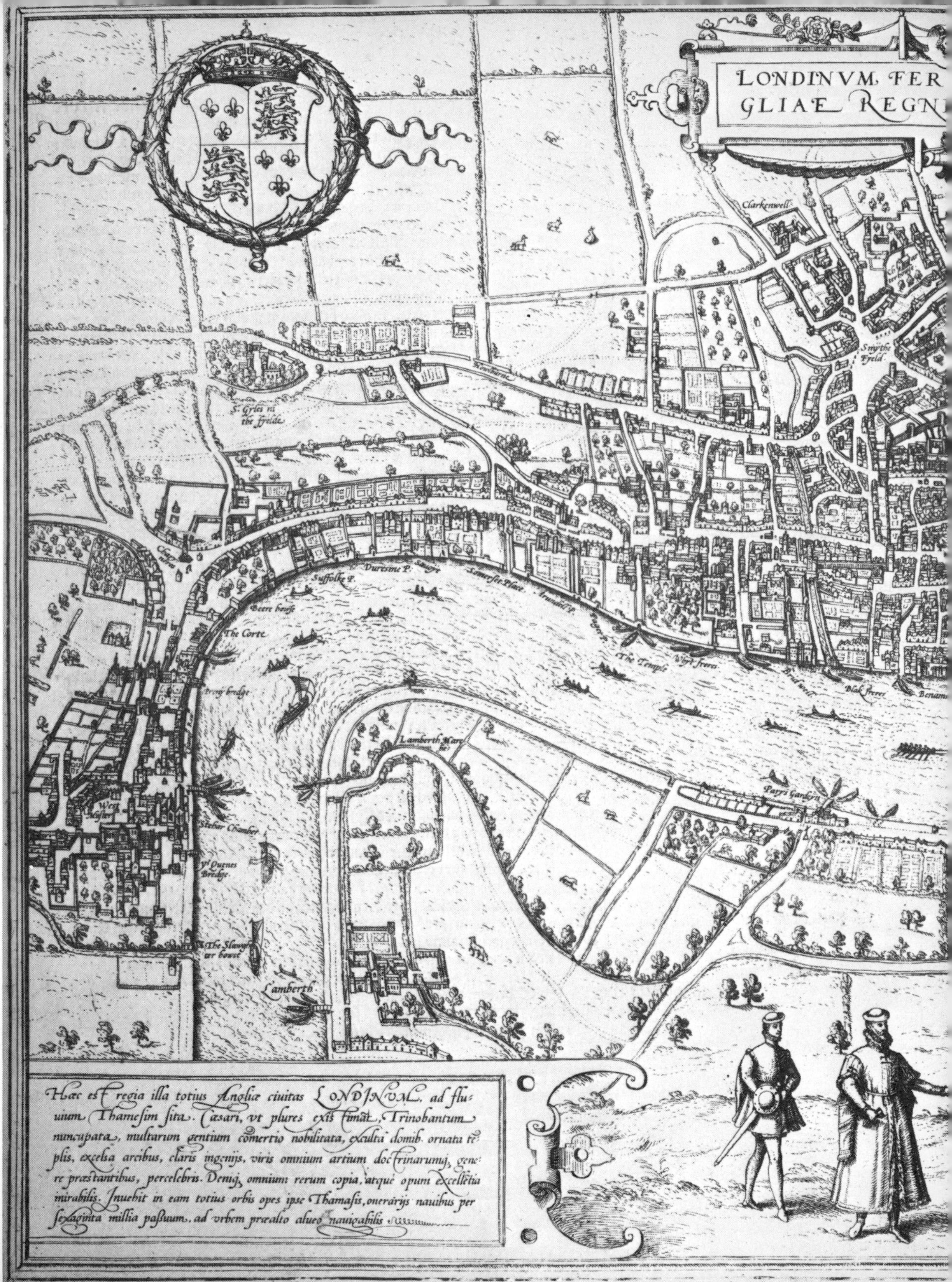

LONDINVM, FER
GLIAE REGN

Clarkenwell

Smythe
Field

S. Gilis in
the fielde

Suffolke P.   Duresme P.   Savoy
                        Somerset Place
                                        Arundell
Beere howse

The Corte   The Temple   White Freeres
Pauls wharfe   Blak Freers
Iront bridge   Beniamin

Lamberth Mary

Baynards
Castle   Parris Garden

Stilleard Chamber

ye Quenes
Bridge

The Slangter
howse

Lamberth

Hæc eſt Regia illa totius Angliæ ciuitas LONDINVM, ad flu:
uium Thameſim ſita, Cæſari, vt plures exiſtimāt, Trinobantum
nuncupata, multarum gentium cōmertio nobilitata, exculta domib. ornata tē
plis, excelſa arcibus, claris ingenijs, viris omnium artium doctrinarumꝗ, gene
re præſtantibus, percelebris. Deniꝗ, omnium rerum copia, atꝗ opum excellētia
mirabilis. Inuehit in eam totius orbis opes ipse Thameſis, onerarijs nauibus per
ſexaginta millia paſſuum, ad vrbem præalto alueo nauigabilis.

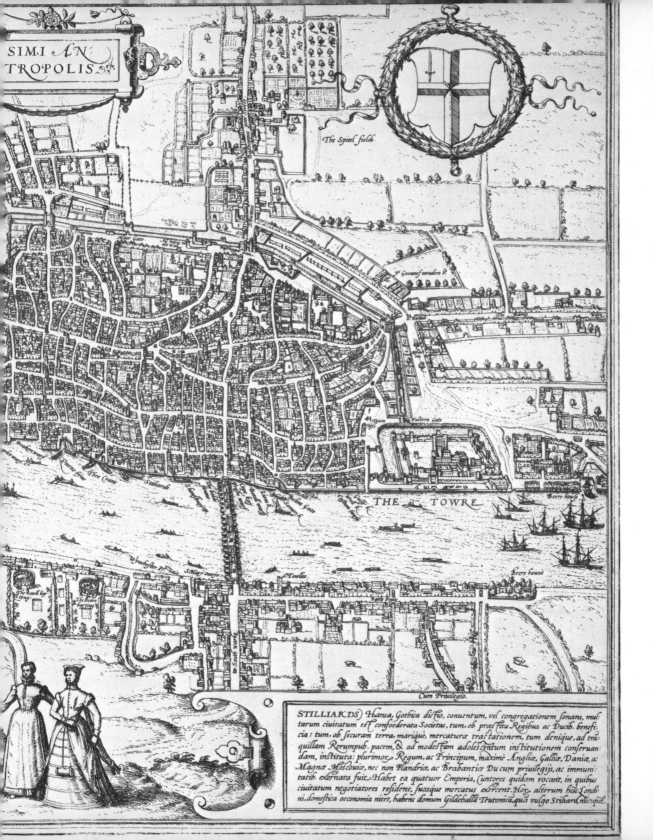

SIMI AN-
TROPOLIS

The Spitel fields.

ye Gownes onuders

Postern Gate

THE TOWRE

Beere house

Towells

Beere howse

Cum Priuilegio.

STILLIARDS) Hansa, Gothica dictio, conuentum, vel congregationem sonans, multarum ciuitatum est confoederata Societas, tum, ob praestita Regibus, ac Ducib. benefi-
cia: tum, ob securam terra, marique, mercaturae tractationem, tum denique, ad tra-
quillam Rerumpub. pacem, & ad modestam adolescentum institutionem conseruan-
dam, instituta: plurimor. Regum, ac Principum, maximè Angliae, Galliae, Daniae, a-
Magnae Moscouiae, nec non Flandriae, ac Brabantiae Ducum priuilegijs, ac immuni-
tatib. Exornata fuit. Habet ea quatuor Emporia, Cuntores quidam vocant, in quibus
ciuitatum negotiatores resident, suasque mercatus exercent. Hor. alterum hic Londi-
ni, domestica oeconomia nitet, habens domum Gildehallam Teutonicam, quã vulgo Stihard, nũcupat.

of workmen hammering and porters man-handling heavy loads could also be heard. In the narrow streets shoppers pushed by groups of men and women gossiping at street corners and children running errands for their masters. Often a violent quarrel would break out and swords or pistols might be drawn, while a crowd gathered to enjoy the excitement. Sometimes apprentices played football through the streets, for at that time it was not played on a pitch with goalposts. Instead it was a free-for-all in which each player tried to grab the ball for himself. There were no rules, and serious injury and even death sometimes occurred.

Those who wished for quieter amusements could play tennis or the newly-fashionable game of bowls. One of the most entertaining ways of spending an afternoon was to watch a play. As you can see from the drawing, the theatre was partly open to the sky. The audience sat in the galleries around the stage, or even on the stage where everyone could see them if they really wanted to be fashionable. The cheapest seats were on the floor around the stage where the groundlings sat. William Shakespeare was first an actor and then a playwright with one of the big London companies. Although audiences were often noisy and restless, being more interested in the other play-goers or the orange-sellers than

Previous pages: London in the time of Elizabeth. Can you find the following: a bull-ring; a bear-pit; the Tower of London; the docks; Lambeth Palace (where the archbishop lived); old St Paul's Cathedral; the Bridewell Prison; Charing Cross; Westminster; Smithfield Market? How many beer-houses can you find?

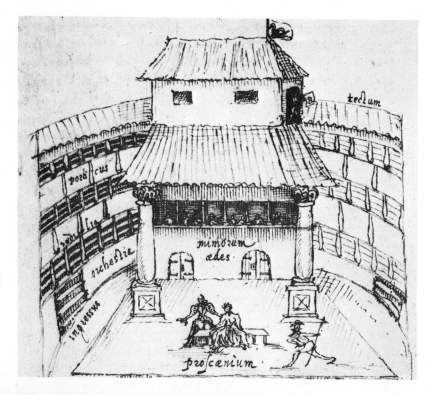

The Swan Theatre in 1596, flying its emblem on the flag. The stage and the area round it where part of the audience stood was open to the sky because of the need for light. There was little scenery; scene changes were announced on placards carried across the stage.

in the performance, Shakespeare's plays were very successful in his own day. Ordinary people enjoyed them for their exciting story as well as for the life-like characters which they showed and the beauty of their poetry. Shakespeare was lucky to have some fine actors to perform his plays, including Richard Burbage, the greatest actor of his day, and some skilful boy actors who took women's parts.

Some people disapproved of the theatre. One writer believed that it led to the spread of the plague, a form of Black Death, which often came to strike fear into the citizens of London. It is interesting to hear his reasons: 'The cause of plague is sin . . . and the cause of sin is plays: therefore the causes of plague are plays.'

The same writer also criticized London's many inns and taverns. The English were famous throughout Europe for their drinking. One of their favourite drinks was sack, a sweet wine which cost over half a crown a gallon, though many still drank ale or beer. Games of cards and dice often started up at the inns and some rogues were able to make a living from their loaded dice or cunningly marked cards. Another favourite trick was to put a mirror behind the victim so that his cards were reflected in it.

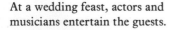

At a wedding feast, actors and musicians entertain the guests.

Fashions in dress

As you can see from the drawings, soft draperies were no longer the fashion. Clothes were elaborate and tight-fitting so that the man or woman of fashion had to seek the services of a good London tailor who could copy the latest styles from Spain and France.

Under their dresses women wore a corselet to give them a flat-chested look, and a farthingale or crinoline to make their skirts stick out. Collars of starched lace called ruffs were also in fashion. Like the queen, wealthy women had dresses of silk, velvet, cloth of gold and silver gauze. Sometimes they were decorated with small rubies, pearls and other gems. Even a woman from the poorer classes might take an interest in fashion and

Miniature of Sir Walter Raleigh. Elaborate hairstyles and ruffs were popular among Elizabethan men.

Costumes of men and women dating from the late sixteenth century.

usually owned two everyday dresses as well as a best dress made of material costing as much as eighteen pence a yard. She would also have a cloak, three or four underskirts and a pair of shoes, which she only wore on special occasions.

Men also took a pride in their clothes. One merchant left clothes which ranged from a red silk gown with a border of velvet worth 60s., and a fur-lined cloak worth the same, to a red cloak worth 4s., and an old satin doublet worth 2s. There were also many fashions for men's hair. The young gallant had a choice of cuts named the 'Spanish', the 'bravado', the 'court', and the 'gentleman's' among others. Beards were also trimmed to the latest style, and the customer was sent away smelling sweet from the soap and oils used by the barber.

A woman's bodice of about 1600. The Elizabethans were very fond of embroidered clothes. The bodice and more examples of embroidered clothes can be seen at the Victoria and Albert Museum.

Houses and furniture

The outside of most London houses would not impress the visitor. It was only the great country houses, such as Hardwick Hall, built by Bess, Countess of Shrewsbury, which showed how well the Elizabethans could use bricks and stone to build a magnificent exterior. Some merchants' houses in the city were built of stone instead of the old clay and wattle, but their simple appearance gave no clue to the magnificence inside.

Tapestries, carpets, cushions and upholstered chairs brought the Elizabethans more comfort than earlier ages had known. One writer tells us that the three changes that old men noticed most were that there were more chimneys, that straw mattresses with a log for the pillow were being replaced by feather beds and pillows, and that plates and spoons were often made of pewter or tin instead of wood. Glassware was often seen in the homes of the rich. Forks were now beginning to be used at table, following the queen's example.

Of course, a poor man could not enjoy all the comforts of the rich, but his life, too, was easier. He might hope to own a trestle-table and benches, a feather bed and a few wooden trenchers. His most precious possessions, however, were still his cow (worth about a pound), his sheep and pigs (worth 5s. each), and his farm produce, such as wheat, hay and cheese.

Above: Hardwick Hall, Derbyshire, built for Elizabeth Shrewsbury in 1590–97.

Below: a sixteenth-century travelling coffer or writing-desk made of oak and covered in leather.

190

Above: a carved oak table and chair. Both date from the first half of the sixteenth century.

Right: a walnut bed dated 1593. The mattress was supported by a network of ropes.

Food

Except in years when the harvests were very bad, most people had enough food, though the poor had very little meat and had to make do with cheese and vegetables. They ate when they had the time, but the upper classes had breakfast when they rose about six, dinner, the main meal of the day, at eleven and supper at six in the evening.

Here is what one wealthy young man and his guests enjoyed at his lodgings one night:

Butter 4d., beef 14d., leg of mutton 18d., veal 22d., 3 quarts of strawberries 16d., 2 lbs. of cherries 20d., ½ lb. of musk confects (sweets) 10d., ½ lb. violet confects 11d., oranges 3d., 2 lemons 6d., bread 8d., beer 9d.

A child's life

The children of Elizabethan England shared in the greater comfort and better food enjoyed by adults. Parents were still very strict, however. Lady Jane Grey has left us this picture of her childhood:

For when I am in presence either of father or mother, whether I speak, keep silence, stand or go, eat, drink, be merry or sad, be sewing, playing or dancing, or doing anything else, I must do it . . . so perfectly as God made the world; else I am so sharply taunted, so cruelly threatened, yes presently with pinches, nips and blows . . . that I think myself in Hell.

Yet most children seem to have had fun playing with their friends. There were few toys, and they had to make their own amusements, playing such games as tig, blind-man's-buff, marbles, and follow-my-leader, just as children had done earlier in the Middle Ages.

A nobleman's children were usually taught by a tutor at home and then sent off to learn manners at the home of some other great man. They were sometimes treated just like unpaid servants. Latin, and sometimes Greek, were taught, though English was coming to be the language used in writing learned works as well as in everyday life.

Many boys went from the grammar schools to Oxford and Cambridge for a year or two to complete their education. There they tended to spend their time enjoying themselves and causing riots in the town rather than getting down to sober study. The universities were losing their close links with the Church and fewer students went on to become clergymen, although they all had to be members of the Church of England.

It was becoming harder for a poor boy to get a good education,

A rich Elizabethan family in 1567. The girls in the centre are twins. The children are dressed in the same style of clothes as their parents.

even if he was very intelligent. The monastery schools had come to an end or been turned into grammar schools. A poor boy could not afford the cost of fees and books and might live too far away to travel to school every day. Rich landowners and merchants were not so willing to help as the upper classes had been in the past.

Freedom in Elizabethan England

The English nation had become much more free by the end of the Middle Ages. Men might change their work or the place where they lived. The enterprising merchant or landowner could make money as never before. The queen and her council were even willing to allow freedom of religion to those who kept quiet and did not threaten the safety of the kingdom.

Yet this freedom brought with it new fears. There were some people who grew rich and lived in comfort, but more who grew desperate because they had lost work and home. The government tried to help by passing laws to protect the poor. The result of this was that the middle classes who had supported the Tudors began to turn against them. Already in the reign of Elizabeth the struggle between the Crown and parliament had begun.

Dates to remember

1563   Elizabeth's first Poor Law
1590   Hardwick Hall was begun
1602   Shakespeare's play, *Hamlet*, produced

Things to do

1   To help the fishing industry and the navy the Elizabethans were ordered to eat fish on Wednesdays, Fridays and Saturdays. How would this be agreed on by the queen and council? Describe how orders would be given to see that the decision was carried out.

2   What kind of rogue is described in each of these passages?

(a) . . . with his staff he plucked off their garments which lay upon them to keep them warm, with the coverlet and the sheet, and left them lying asleep, naked saving their shirts and had all away clean.

(b) If they met a woman alone riding to the market either old man or boy that he well knoweth will not resist, such they filch and spoil (rob).

(c) He renewed his face with fresh blood . . . which he carried about him in a bladder, and daubed fresh dirt upon his jerkin, hat and hosen. And so came back again unto the Temple and some-time to the water-side and begged of all them that passed by.

3   Here is a description of a game played in the time of Elizabeth. Can you guess what it is?

Doth not everyone lie in wait for his adversary, seeking to overthrow him and pick him in his nose, though it be upon hard stones . . . ? Sometimes their noses gush with blood, and sometimes hurt in one place, sometimes in another.

4 Find out all you can about the life of William Shakespeare and make a list of his plays. How was a theatre of Shakespeare's time different from a theatre today?

5 Compare the prices of food, clothes and livestock which you find in this chapter with the prices of things now. Which prices have changed least?

Books to read

Christine Price, *Made in the Renaissance*, Bodley Head

Molly Harrison and M. E. Bryant, *The Sixteenth Century*, Allen & Unwin (A Picture Source Book)

Ivor Brown, *Shakespeare and his Time*, Nelson

John Hayes, *London from the Earliest Times to the Present Day*, Black

I. Doncaster, *Elizabethan and Jacobean Home Life*, Longman

After hunting, Elizabethan enjoyed large and elaborate meals in the open air with their servants at hand to provide every comfort.

Chapter 19
Gerard and Wentworth – Catholic and Puritan in the reign of Elizabeth

Religious persecution

Today in Britain religion is not usually a fighting matter. We find it difficult to understand an age in which men were denied the right to worship as they wished. In the sixteenth century, however, beliefs which were different from those of the head of a state could easily lead to treason. A change of religion often went with a change of ruler.

When Elizabeth came to the throne in 1558, she soon made it clear that she was to be a moderate Protestant. On being met by monks with candles at the state opening of parliament, she cried angrily, 'Away with those torches, for we see well enough.' She passed an Act which made her Governor of the Church as well as the State, but she did not claim the title of 'Supreme Head' as her father had done. Archbishop Cranmer's Prayer Book was the only one to be used in churches. Those who did not attend services were to be fined. Priests and bishops who could not agree were expelled from the Church.

Gerard's early life

John Gerard was born into a Catholic family six years after these changes were made. Although Elizabeth's spies usually knew who the Catholics were, they were often left in peace. The fines for not going to church were not demanded from them so often that they would be ruined. After 1570 when a new and energetic Pope tried to send missionaries to convert England, and seemed to encourage plots against the queen, the English Catholics begged to be left alone. In letters to Rome they pointed out that while they remained loyal subjects, they were allowed to keep their religion.

Gerard's father was not one of these. He was in a plot to rescue the Catholic Mary, Queen of Scots, and put her on the throne. Even so he got permission for his son to go to France for his schooling, which meant that he had a Catholic education. Once on a visit home the boy was put in prison for a time. There he saw a Catholic priest who had been kept working on a treadmill. He wrote:

Popish plots, 1605. The government approved of pictures like these because they showed the wickedness of Catholics and the punishments that awaited them. Among the plots are: 1. The rebellion of the northern earls in 1569. 3. The beginning of an expedition against Elizabeth by Thomas Stukeley in 1578. 9. An attempt by Parry, a member of parliament, to kill the queen. 10. The Babington plot. 12. The Armada. 13. A plot by Elizabeth's Jewish doctor, Lopez, to poison her. This was uncovered by the Earl of Essex and the queen did not really believe it. 14. The rebellion of the Earl of Tyrone in Ireland.

There was nothing left of him except skin and bone and I cannot remember seeing anything like it – lice swarmed on him like ants on a
mole-hill, but he bore it in patience.

Far from being put off by what he had seen, Gerard decided to
become a Jesuit priest. The Jesuits were the followers of the
Spaniard, Ignatius Loyola, whose aim was to win back Protestant
countries to the Catholic faith. He went to the Jesuit College at
Douai where young men were trained to die as well as live for
their faith. To help them there were pictures on the walls showing
Christian martyrs.

A Catholic priest on the run

In 1588, the year in which Philip of Spain sent his great fleet
to conquer England for the Catholic Church, Gerard set out
secretly for England. To be caught and recognized as a priest
meant death. He landed on a rainy autumn night. At last he took
shelter in a wood, for as he wandered near houses in the dark he
set the dogs barking. After several days he reached London and
was sent to Norfolk by his superiors. There he stayed with a
Catholic family. He dressed simply, as a man of moderate wealth,
and made several converts among those he came to know. Once
on a journey to the north he was at Baddesley Clinton when the

Baddesley Clinton, showing a
back exit which may have been
known to Gerard.

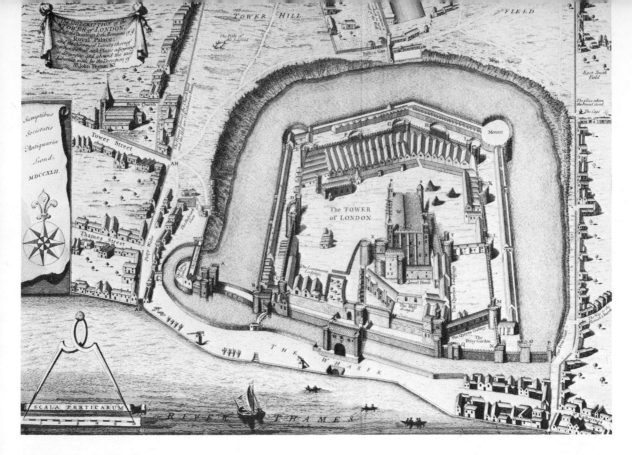

The Tower of London in 1597. Both Gerard and Wentworth were imprisoned here.

house was searched. Like most Catholic houses of the time, the manor had a priest-hole. For four hours Gerard and the others stood with their feet in water, for the hiding place was below ground level. At last the searchers went away disappointed.

Imprisonment and torture

Gerard was finally betrayed by a traitor. He was put into the Tower of London and tortured to obtain a full confession. In a dark, underground room he was hung by chains from the top of a pillar so that his feet hung off the ground. Several times he fainted with the pain. Steps were placed under him until he came round and began to pray. Then the support was taken from him again. In the evening, so Gerard tells us, he was asked:

'Are you ready now to obey the queen and her Council?' I answered, 'You want me to do what is sinful. I will not do it.' In a rage he suddenly turned his back on me and strode from the room, shouting angrily in a loud voice, 'Then hang there until you rot from the pillar.'

It must have been a bad moment for Gerard. However, he was

199

soon cut down. After more torture he thought of a way of escape. With a friend he slid down a weighted rope to the river where a boat was waiting. So Gerard escaped the dreadful fate of being hanged, drawn and quartered. He was still free and in England when the queen died.

The Puritan danger

Catholics, such as Gerard, were not tolerated because they often plotted to replace Elizabeth with another ruler of their own faith. A Puritan, such as Peter Wentworth, believed they were doing the devil's work. Many times in the House of Commons he risked the queen's anger and demanded more harshness towards them, and the death of Mary Stuart whom they wanted as queen. The Puritans wanted no other ruler but Elizabeth. They saw that the Tudors had made changes in religion by Act of Parliament. Now they wanted parliament, led by the Puritan members of the House of Commons to make reforms in the Church of England. Elizabeth and her councillors came to regard the Puritans as a dangerous nuisance because they challenged her right to control the Church and dared to criticize her government.

Scene of torture. This engraving from Foxe's *Book of Martyrs* shows the torture of Protestants by Catholics, but both sides used the same methods.

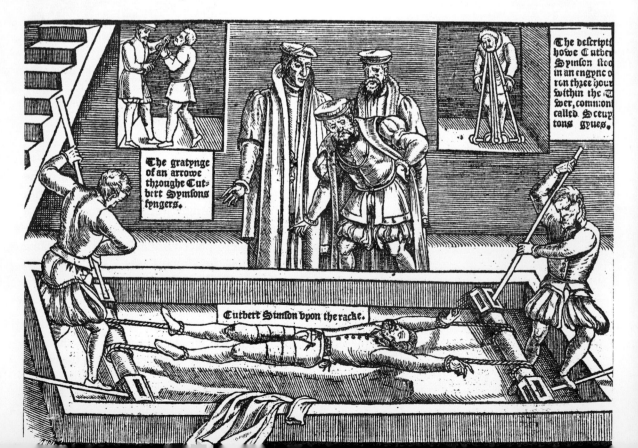

The effects of persecution. By the end of Elizabeth's reign, some Puritans were leaving England for Holland and Germany, where they could worship freely.

A Puritan's ideas

Peter Wentworth was born into a wealthy family of the sort which, as we have seen, had come to dislike the government's attempts to help the poor and unemployed. As a young man he studied law, but until he was forty-seven he lived the life of a country gentleman. Then he became so worried by the danger of a successful Catholic plot that he went into Parliament as the member for Tregony in Cornwall.

Some of the ideas of Wentworth and his friends came from John Calvin. He believed that as some men were damned from birth, so others were the chosen people of God, and must show this by their way of life. The Puritans dressed soberly and were noted for their high standard of behaviour. They avoided drink, gambling and the theatre, and protested against the games and dancing which, to them, ruined the sabbath, God's day of rest. The Puritans came to prefer their own services to those of the Prayer Book, and to hate the bishops who made them use it. Many of the outward things to be seen in the Church offended them as unnecessary. They saw no need for making the sign of the cross on the child's forehead at baptism or for having a ring as a sign of marriage.

Wentworth the rebel

Wentworth supported his friends in parliament who tried to pass bills to reform the Church and its worship. He even dared to demand that the queen should name a Protestant prince to succeed to the throne after her death. At a time when Elizabeth was held in the highest respect the daring Wentworth shocked the House of Commons by declaring, 'None is without fault, not our noble queen,' and later threatened her with 'ten thousand hells in your soul.' Not surprisingly, he was several times put in prison not only by Elizabeth herself, but also at the command of the other members of parliament who were horrified at his behaviour.

Wentworth complained that they were too easily frightened by the queen's councillors who sat in the Commons. Some members of parliament watched to see which way they voted and then did the same. Sometimes a man who did not was called before the council and came back looking so dazed and frightened that the others refused to follow Wentworth's lead. He took to holding meetings of his own party to prepare a plan of action, but these were discovered and he was once more put in prison where he died, still protesting his loyalty to the queen.

We must remember that Wentworth, like Gerard, wanted freedom for his own views but not for the opinions of others. The queen was more tolerant of the Catholics and Puritans than they were of each other or of the Church of England. Yet Wentworth's demands for freedom of speech in parliament are still stirring today. His belief that it was 'the only salve to heal the sores of the commonwealth,' was echoed in the next century when the Puritan members of parliament went to war with their king.

Dates to remember

1588   Gerard arrived in England
1593   Wentworth was imprisoned for the last time

Things to do

1   Make a play out of Gerard's adventures.
2   Many different kinds of Christians, apart from Roman Catholics and members of the Church of England, live in Britain today. Make a list of them and find out what you can about their beliefs.
3   Here is a Puritan tale. Read it through and answer these questions:
    (a) What sins did the eight men commit?
    (b) What was the Puritan idea of punishment for sin?
    (c) Make up a Puritan tale for today in which modern sins are suitably punished.

There were dwelling eight men . . . all of which would needs go to the tavern upon the Sabbath Day in the morning very early in contempt of the Lord and his Sabbath. And coming to the house of one Anthony Hage, an honest goodly man who kept an inn in the same town, called for drink. The host told them they should have none . . . and counselled them to hear the word of God preached. But they denied, saying that they 'loathed that kind of exercise.' The good host . . . went to the sermon as duty did bind him, who being gone, they fell to cursing . . . 'The devil break our necks if we depart hence this day either quick or dead, till we have some wine.' Straightway the devil appeared unto them in the likeness of a young man, bringing in his hand a flagon of wine and saying, 'Good fellows be merry, for ye shall have wine enough, for ye seem lusty lads and I hope you will pay me well,' who unthinkingly answered, that they would pay him or else bet their necks on it, yea their bodies and souls rather than fail. . . . At last the devil, their host, told them they must needs pay the bill, whereat their hearts grew cold. But the devil, comforting them, said, 'Be of good cheer, for now you must drink boiling lead, pitch and brimstone with me in the pit of Hell for evermore!' . . . And before they could call for Mercy and Grace, the devil prevented them, and break their necks asunder and threw most horrible flames of fire flashing from their mouths.

Book to read

Agnes Allen, *The Story of our Parliament*, Faber

A letter from Peter Wentworth dated 20 July 1597 from the Tower. He wrote to Sir Robert Cecil reminding him that he had been in prison for four years and asking for release because he was sick and old. Although the Cecil family was sympathetic to the Puritan party, Wentworth's request was refused and he died soon afterwards.

Chapter 20
Richard Hakluyt and the beginnings of the British Empire

Hakluyt's interest in exploration

While he was still a schoolboy, Richard Hakluyt visited his cousin. Lying open on a table in the room were a few geography books and a map of the world. Seeing the boy's interest in them, his cousin began to talk of the distant lands and seas which the famous seamen of the Renaissance had reached. From this day the course of Hakluyt's life was changed.

It is true that he became a clergyman and never sailed farther than across the English Channel to France. Yet his delight in the travel of others was so great that he spent much of his life finding out all he could about the explorers of his time. More than anything else he wanted to write a book which would show the other nations of Europe that Elizabeth's England could boast the finest, most courageous sailors in the world.

The race for new lands overseas

At first England had been left behind in the competition for newly discovered lands in Africa and America. Apart from John Cabot who sailed to Newfoundland in the reign of Henry VII, English kings had employed no seamen of the quality of Columbus, da Gama and Magellan, who did so much to make Spain and Portugal rich and powerful. Yet as England grew more peaceful under Tudor rule, men felt willing to explore the world and take the risk of leaving their homes. Merchants were also ready to risk money in fitting out expeditions which might lead to new trade. By the middle of the sixteenth century the English had entered the race to reach and claim lands overseas.

Conditions aboard ship

Explorers were helped by improvements in the ships they sailed in. Henry VIII had increased the size of the navy and replaced many of the clumsy carracks with swift, slender galleons which were partly copied from the galleys of the Mediterranean. As you can see from the drawing, they were not large, but they were well-balanced and could be easily manoeuvred to make the best use of wind and weather. Growing knowledge of the movements of the sun and stars, and the use of the astrolabe and cross-staff made

Henry Grace a Dieu, a carrack
built for Henry VIII in 1514.
(Compare with the carrack on
page 78.)

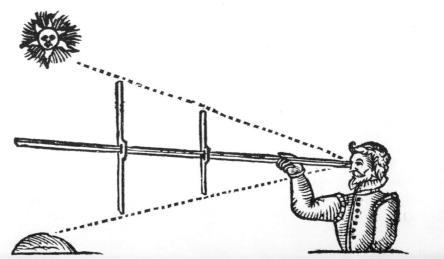

A navigator using a cross-staff
to plot his position and course
by the sun.

it simpler for navigators to fix the right course and position of the ship.

Still life on board remained full of hardship. The men were packed in together without sanitation or good water supply. Their food for a day might be a biscuit, a gallon of beer, and 2 lb. of salt beef or pork, or butter with cheese. Often food went bad, and the crew ended a long voyage in near starvation. Since there were no fresh vegetables on board, many of the men died of scurvy, which is described in one of the voyages in Hakluyt's book:

Their gums waxe (grow) great, and swell, and they are fain to cut them away. Their legs swell and all the body becometh sore, and so benumbed that they cannot stir hand nor foot.

It was quite usual for a ship to lose half its crew from disease.

Even for those who remained healthy, life was hard. The crew worked on deck or in the rigging in all weathers. Punishments for those who were careless or disobedient included flogging, ducking from the yard-arm, being put in irons, and keel-hauling in which the victim was dragged under water beneath the length of the whole ship. Hakluyt tells us of the fate of Thomas Doughtie who seems to have tried to organize a mutiny against Drake on his voyage round the world. He was beheaded as a warning to the rest of the crew.

Vasco da Gama.

Why explorers set out

The risks of exploration could bring big rewards. Drake came home in 1580 with loot taken from the Spaniards which was worth half a million pounds. His main aim had been to discover a north-west passage through the seas of North America to the land of Cathay (China) and the islands of the East where precious spices, silks and jewels were to be found.

In contrast, other explorers set out not so much to make money as to study 'The works of the Lord and his wonders in the deep', in the words of the psalm which Hakluyt loved so well. Compared with Mandeville, the Elizabethan traveller was a truthful and accurate observer of the people and places he visited. Much of what he wrote shows a scientific interest in plants, birds and animals and would not be out of place in a modern geography book.

Sir Francis Drake.

The North-West Passage

Some of the most interesting stories in Hakluyt's book are about the search for a quick sea route to the east by way of North

• • • • Columbus 1492-93
------ da Gama 1497-98
-·-·- Cabot 1498
——— Magellan 1519-23
- - - - - Chancellor 1553-54
········ Jenkinson 1557-61
━━━ Frobisher 1576-78
– – – Drake 1577-80
▪▪▪▪ Fitch 1583

European exploration in
Tudor times.

America. This would avoid the long sea voyage round the Cape
of Good Hope, which was used by rival merchants from Spain and
Holland.

In 1576 Martin Frobisher set out to explore the seas of northern
Canada. He had to turn back from 'mountains of ice' without
finding the passage he was looking for. Several times he met
hostile natives and was once wounded in the backside by an
arrow as he scrambled to escape. He noticed how they used some
dogs to draw sledges and others to eat. When a man and woman
were taken prisoner, the crew watched their behaviour carefully
and were touched to see the way the two captives learned to care
for and protect each other. At one point on the voyage, cliffs which
seemed to be made of gold were sighted, but they proved to be no
better than black lead. Some stones from them were carried home,
but were found to be so worthless that they were used to mend a
road.

John Davis made three further attempts to find the North-
West Passage, but he failed to notice the Hudson Strait and was
driven back by the ice which could rip a ship in two and by the
cold which left his crew weak and pale. Unlike Frobisher, Davis
was quite friendly to the Eskimos in spite of their habit of

stealing anything they could lay their hands on. Even lamps, ropes and an anchor disappeared. He describes their broad faces, with small eyes and wide mouths, and their small hands and feet. Davis also began a dictionary of useful Eskimo words, such as the greeting '*Ylyaoute*', which meant 'I mean no harm', '*ugnera*' – 'my son', '*nugo*' – 'no', and '*cany-glow*' – 'kiss me'.

A battle between Frobisher and the Eskimos.

The first English colonists

Sir Humphrey Gilbert, who encouraged the search for the North-West Passage, also believed that settlements should be begun in North America. These would provide raw materials for the mother country and take in exchange manufactured goods, especially cloth, the chief English export. In 1583 he set out to study the conditions in Newfoundland, but he never returned. His ship

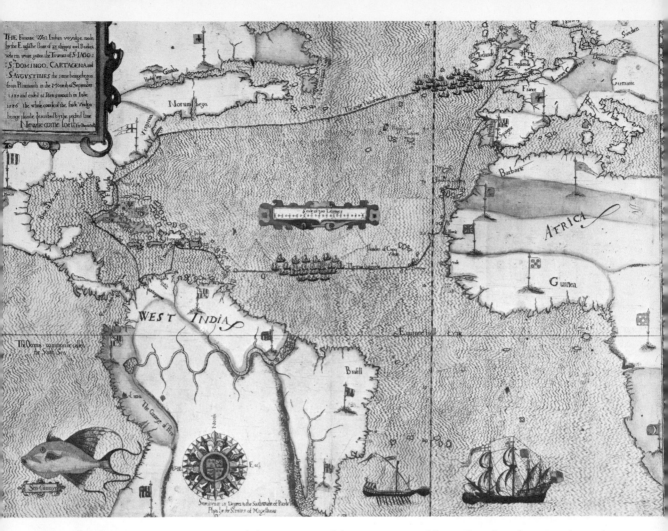

Drake's route to the West Indies, 1583–86. Flags mark the possessions of different countries. Compared to the map on page 79, this is accurate and detailed.

was driven aground in a storm and he refused a place on the only boat which could be launched, as this would mean leaving most of his men. The survivors saw the lights of the ship suddenly disappear, and then drifted for six days without food or water until they came ashore safely.

The other attempt to begin a settlement in North America was organized by Sir Walter Raleigh. A first voyage to Virginia, as the new colony was to be called, showed it to be a beautiful and fertile land. In its warm climate grew grapes, melons, walnuts, cucumbers, peas, roots (potatoes), corn and wheat. Meat was provided by hares, rabbits and deer. Huge cedars gave promise of wood for building.

And yet the two attempts to begin a settlement there failed. The first group ran out of supplies to see them through the winter and were taken home by Drake. The second group fared even worse. Soon after they landed one of them became separated from the rest while hunting crabs. He was shot through with sixteen arrows and his head was beaten in. In spite of this the settlers decided to stay, but when their leader returned from England with more supplies, there was no trace of them. Starvation or the Indians had destroyed every one.

A visit to Russia

Before a search was made for the North-West Passage in America, English explorers had been looking for a route to the East along the north coast of Russia. The ice and bitter weather made such a voyage impossible, but journeys were made overland through Russia to Persia and the other lands of Asia.

Barents' sailors fleeing from the dangers of pack-ice to their ship. Barents was a Dutchman who explored the North-East Passage and the sea that has been named after him, but died before reaching home (1597).

As Edward VI lay dying, Richard Chancellor set out on a voyage which took him to Moscow where he made a trade treaty with the Tsar on behalf of the ruler of England. The tallow, hides, oil, tar and timber which came from Russia were very welcome because trade in these goods in the Baltic area was in the hands of the German merchants.

Hakluyt prints a good account of what Russia was like in the days of Tsar Ivan the Terrible. The Englishman visited Moscow with its great fortress, the Kremlin, and reported that,

Their streets and ways are not paved with stone as ours are. The walls of their houses are of wood. The rooves for the most part are covered with shingle boards. There is hard by the city a very fair castle, strong and furnished with artillery, whereunto the city is joined

Moscow in 1573, with the Kremlin surrounded by a wall, and the river Moscva *(left)*.

directly towards the North with a brick wall. The walls of the castle are built with brick and are in breadth or thickness eighteen foot. This castle hath on the one side a dry ditch and on the other the river Moscva.

Though they were determined not to find anything in Russia better than at home, the English visitors were impressed by the golden robes of the Tsar and his nobles, his magnificent gold plate, and the toughness of the Russian soldiers who hung up their cloaks against the wind and lay down near their horses on the hard ground with only a small fire to warm them in the bitterly cold weather. Their only food was a little oatmeal and water. Chancellor and his friends were surprised that most Russians knew so little about the Christian faith and shocked by the Russian law which did not hang a thief at once as in England. Instead, he was put in prison the first time he stole. The second time he was branded and had his nose cut off. The third time he was hanged.

Trade with the East

Later, another traveller, Jenkinson, made a journey through Russia to Persia, where he met the Shah and managed to begin trade with the Persians. This ended when English merchants suddenly found it possible to do business in the Levant, the eastern Mediterranean, again. Earlier, all trade in this area had been stopped by attacks from pirates and the hostility of the Turks who ruled there. However, in 1578 William Harborne set out bravely to the Sultan's court and returned in triumph with an agreement which allowed English merchants to trade in sweet wines, olives and currants.

Encouraged by this, a small expedition led by John Newbery and Ralph Fitch, sailed for Jaffa and then made their way overland to the Indian port of Goa. Fitch went on by himself and reached Bengal, Burma and Malacca before returning home. His great journey led to the setting up of the East India Company to begin trade in the area.

What Hakluyt's book describes is not just a number of voyages but the beginning of England's empire in America and India. The first attempts to begin colonies had been made and the lesson had been learnt that more careful planning and a better type of settler were needed to succeed. The British navy, which played such a large part in gaining and keeping lands overseas in the coming centuries, was now beginning to show its strength. Hakluyt points out that never before the reign of Elizabeth had the countries of the world seen the might and wealth of England. Britain was entering the seventeenth century, not as a backward little island on the edge of the world, but as a growing power at its centre.

Dates to remember

1576   Frobisher's first voyage in search of the North-West Passage

1577–80   Drake sailed round the world

1587   The second settlement in Virginia

1600   The East India Company began

Things to do

1   Trace the routes of the explorers Columbus, Magellan and da Gama on the map, and find out all you can about their careers.

2   Compare the drawing of Henry VIII's ship, the *Henry Grace à Dieu*, with the drawing of a medieval carrack on page 78, and make a list of the differences between them.

3   Find out all you can about Russia in the reign of Ivan the Terrible and compare it with the information brought back by Chancellor and his companions.

4   Read these poems which tell of the courage and daring of Elizabethan seamen: *The Revenge*, by Tennyson, *Drake's Drum*, by Newbolt, *The Armada*, by Macaulay.

Books to read

Geoffrey Trease, *Fortune my Foe, Sir Walter Raleigh*, Methuen

P. Dawlish, *Martin Frobisher*, Oxford University Press

L. A. Kent, *He went with Christopher Columbus*, Harrap

            He went with Magellan, Harrap

            He went with Vasco Da Gama, Harrap

P. Dawlish, *He went with Drake*, Harrap

Index

Numbers listed in italics (e.g. *15*) refer to the captions of illustrations and maps. fl. *stands for* flourished. d. *stands for* died.

Acre, Siege of (1191), 72–3
Adelard of Bath (fl.12th century), 115
Adrian IV, Pope (d.1159), 115
Aetius (d.454), 12, 16
Agincourt, Battle of (1415), 122, *127*
Aidan St (d.651), 20
Air photography, 6, *7*
Alcuin (735–804), 41
Alexander III, King of Scotland (1241–85), 91
Alexander III, Pope (d.1181), 62
Alfred, King of Wessex (849–901), 47–9
America,
  colonies in, 208–10
  discovery of, 45, 148, 204
  search for North-West passage, 206–8
Angles, 13
  see also Barbarian invasion of Britain
Anne Boleyn, Queen (1507–36), 139, *139–40*, 142, 154, *167*, 168
Anne of Cleves, Queen (1515–57), *146*, *167*
Apprenticeship, 111, 113, 182
Archaeology, 6–8
Arderne, John of (fl.1370), 116
Armada, 174–7
Arsuf, Battle of (1191), 74
Arthur, King (fl.500), 14–16
Ascham, Roger (1515–68), 170
Ashdown, Battle of (871), 47
Aske, Robert (d.1537), 146
Astronomy, 41, 80, 118, 149
Augustine, St (d.604), 19–20, 26, 48

Babington, Anthony (1561–86), 173, *197*
Bacon, Roger (1214–94), 116
Ball, John (d.1381), 130, *131*, 133
Balliol, John, King of Scotland (1249–1315), 91
Bannockburn, Battle of (1314), 92, 120
Barbarian invasion of Britain, 12–16
Barons, 57, 60, 84–6

Bayeux Tapestry, 50, *51–5*
Becket, Thomas, St (1118?–70), 60–5, *62–5*, 69
Bede (673–735), 25, 28, 41–2, 48
Benedict, St (480?–543?), 22, 25–6, 143
Beowulf, 33
Bernard, St (1090–1153), 65
Bess, Countess of Shrewsbury (1518–1608), 190
Black Death, 128–9, 134, 187
Black Prince, Edward (1330–76), 121
Boniface, St (680–755), 40, 42
Britons,
  helped by Arthur, 15
  massacred, 14
  pushed westwards, 16
  sufferings after Romans left, 12
Bruce, Robert, King of Scotland (1274–1329), 92
Building, *110–11*
Byzantium, 12

Cabot, John (1450–98), 204, *207*
Caedmon (fl.670), 25
Calvin, John (1509–64), 162, 172
Cannon, *78*, 121, *124*
Canterbury Cathedral, 60, 64, *66*
Canute (994?–1035), 50
Castles, *90*, *97*, 98
Catherine of Aragon, Queen (1485–1536), *139*, *167*
Catherine Howard, Queen (d.1542), 158, *167*
Catherine Parr, Queen (1512–48), *167*, 168
Catholics, in Elizabeth's reign, 196–200
Caxton, William (1422?–91), *148*
Cecil, William (1520–98), 178–9
Celtic Christians, 19–20
Chancellor, Richard (d.1556), *207*, 211–12
Charles the Great, Emperor (742?–814) 40–2
Charles V, Emperor (1500–58), 139, 159
Charles VI, King of France (1368–1422), 122–3
Charles VII, King of France (1403–61), 123–5
Chaucer, Geoffrey (1340?–1400), 114, 118–19
China, 81, *82*, 206
Chippenham, Treaty of (878), 47
Christian faith, 21–2, 26
Church architecture,

  Decorated, *67*
  Early English, *66*
  Norman, *66*
  Perpendicular, *67*
  Saxon, *57*
Church of England, 166
Cistercian monks, 65
Clothes, 34, *35*, *99*, 104, 188–9
Cloth industry, *110*, 182
Coifi (fl. 7th century), 27
Colet, John (1467?–1519), 151
Colonies, 208–10
Columba, St (521–97), 19, *20*
Columbus, Christopher (1446?–1506), 148, 156, *207*
Constantinople, 12, 148
Conversion of England,
  by Augustine, 19
  by Celtic Christians, 19–20
Copernicus, Nicolas (1473–1543), 149, 156
Council, The
  fight for power in, 136
  in Magna Carta, 85
  in medieval times, 94
  in Saxon times, 28
  under Elizabeth I, 178–9, 194
Cranmer, Thomas, Archbishop (1489–1556), 158, 160–6, 196
Crécy, Battle of (1346), 120
Crime, 96, *119*, 181–2
Cromwell, Thomas (1485?–1540), 136, 141–4, 146–7
Crossbows, *91*, 120
Crusades,
  First (1095–9), 70–1
  reasons for, 71–2
  results of, 75, 78
  Third (1189–92), 72–6

Danelaw, 48, 49
Danes, 44–9
Darnley, Henry Stewart, Earl of (1545–67), 172
Dauphin (Charles VII of France), (1403–61), 123–5
David, St (d.601?), 19
Davis, John (1550?–1605), 207–8
Dissolution of the monasteries, 143–7

Domesday Book, 56–8, *56, 58*
Dominic, St (1170–1221), 68
Drake, Sir Francis (1540?–96), 172, 182, 206, *206, 209*, 213
Dress, *91,* 104, 188–9

East India Company, 212–13
Edington, Battle of (878), 47, 49
Education, *25,* 114–15, 151, 192–3
Edward the Confessor (d.1066), 50, *51*
Edward the Elder (d.924), 49
Edward I (1239–1307),
  and Ireland, 86, 88
  and Parliament, 86
  and Scotland, 90–2
  and Wales, 88–90
Edward II (1284–1327), 90, 92, 94, 120
Edward III (1312–77), 120–1, 127
Edward IV (1442–83), *135,* 136
Edward V (1470–83?), *135*
Edward VI (1537–53), *162,* 163
Eleanor of Aquitaine, Queen (1122?–1204), 70
Elizabeth I (1533–1603),
  and Mary, Queen of Scots, 172–4
  and Spain, 172, 174–6
  appearance and manner, 169–70, 177
  death, 176
  government, 178–9
  religious policy, 166, 168
  suitors, 171–2
Elizabeth of York, Queen (1465–1503), *135,* 136
Enclosure, *6,* 180–1
Entertainments, 33, 46, 100–1, 113, 186–7
Erasmus, Desiderius (1466?–1536), 151
Eskimoes, 207–8
Essex, Robert Devereux, Earl of (1567–1601), 176
Ethelbert, King of Kent (552?–616), 19
Ethelred, King of Wessex (d.871), 47
Ethelred the Redeless, King of England (968?–1016), 50
Evesham, Battle of (1265), 85
Executions, *30, 126, 132, 144, 164–5, 173, 197*

Fairs, 113
Falkirk, Battle of (1298), 92

Farming, 28, 34–6, 106, *108*, 109, 129, 180–1
Feasting, 100, 104
  see also Entertainment *and* Food
Feudal System, 57
Fitch, Ralph (fl.1583–1606), *207*, 212
Fitz Urse, Reginald (fl.1170), 63–4
Flanders, 86, 120
Food, 33–4, 36, 94, *100*, 104–6, 128, 192
Foxe, John (1516–87), 165
France, Wars with, *see* Hundred Years War
Francis, St (1181–1226), 65, 69
Friars, *68*
  Dominican, 68
  Franciscan, 65, 69, 130
Frobisher, Martin (1535?–94), 207, 213
Froissart, Jean (1335?–83), 127
Furniture, 102–3, 106, 190–1

Gama, Vasco da, 204, *206*
Geoffrey of Monmouth (1100?–54), 15
Gerard, John (1564–1637), 196, 198–200, 202
Gilbert, Humphrey (1539?–83), 208–9
Government,
  Medieval, 94
  Saxon, 28–30
  Tudor, 178–9
Great Charter (Magna Carta), *84*, 84–6
Greek learning, 25, 41, 115, 148
Gregory the Great, Pope (540?–604), 19, 48
Gregory VII, Pope (1023?–85), 60
Grey, Lady Jane, Queen (1537–54), 163, *167*, 192
Guesclin, Bertrand du (d.1380), 121
Guilds, 111, 113, 182
Guthrum, King of East Anglia (d.890), 48

Hairdressing, *104*
Hakluyt, Richard (1552?–1616), 204–12
Hales, Robert (d.1381), 131–2
Halfdan (fl.865), 46
Hampton Court, 139, *140*, 153, *154–5*
Harborne, William (d.1617), 212
Hardwick Hall, *190*, 194
Harold, King of the English (1022?–66), 50–6

Hastings, Battle of (1066), 54–6
Henry IV, Emperor of Germany (1050–1106), 60
Henry I (1068–1135), 115
Henry II (1133–89),
  and barons, 60
  and Becket, 60–3, 65
  conquest of Ireland, 86
  justice, 96
Henry III (1207–72), 85, 90
Henry IV (1367–1413), 122, *135*
Henry V (1387–1422), 122, *123, 135*
Henry VI (1421–71), *135*, 136
Henry VII (1457–1509), 134, *135*, 136, *137*, 204
Henry VIII (1491–1547),
  and Cromwell, 141–3
  and Wolsey, 137–41
  dissolution of the monastries, 143–7
  Reformation under, 161–2, 166
  Renaissance under, 148–57
Hereward the Wake (fl.1070–1), 56
Holbein, Hans (1497–1543), *149*, 153
Homage, 57, *70*
Homes, 34–6, *102*, 106, 110, 190
Houses, *see* Homes
Howard, Lord William, Admiral (1510?–1573), 174
Hundred Years War (1337–1453),
  Edward III in, 120–1
  French revival, 121
  Henry V's success, 122–3
  Joan of Arc in, 123–6
  peace at end of, 126
Hunting 33, 99

India, 80–1, 212
Indulgences, 158–60
Iona, *20*
Ireland,
  Christians in, 19
  conquest of by England, 86
  Edward I and, 88
  Elizabeth and, 176
Ivar the Boneless (fl.865), 46

Jane Seymour, Queen (1509?–37), 162, *167*
Jenkinson, Anthony (d.1611), *207*, 212
Jesuits, 198
Joan of Arc (1412–31), 123–7
John, King (1167?–1216), 70, 75–6, 84, 92
John of Gaunt, Duke of Lancaster (1540–99), 130, 132
Justice, 30–2, 94–6, 138–9
Jutes, 13

Koran, *76*

Lanfranc, Archbishop (1005?–89), 10–11, 57
Langland, William (1330?–1400?), 128
Latin (Roman) learning, 25, 41, 148
Law courts, 94–6, 138–9
Leicester, Robert Dudley, Earl of (1532?–88), 172, *172*
Leonardo da Vinci (1452–1519), *150, 151*
Lindisfarne Gospels, *24–25*
Livery and Maintenance, Act of (1504), 139
Llewellyn, Prince of Gwynedd (d.1282), 89–90
Lollards, 130
London,
  in 1381, *131*
  in Elizabeth's reign, 182–7
Longbows, *91*, 120
Loyola, Ignatius (1491–1556), 198
Luther, Martin (1483–1546), 152, 158–61, 166

Machiavelli, Niccolo (1469–1527), 154
Magellan, Ferdinand (1480?–1521), 148, 204, *207*
Magna Carta, *84*, 84–6
Mandeville, Sir John (fl.1322), *80*, 80–3
Manors, 6, 57, *102*
Markets, 113
Marriage, 34, 103–4
Mary I (1516–58), 139, 143, 163, 165, 168
Mary Stuart, Queen of Scots (1542–87), 172–4, 196, 200
Matilda, Empress (1102–67), *59*, 60, 168
Medicine, 42, 116–18, 128, 149
Medina, Sidonia (fl.1588), 175
Medrod or Medraut (fl.500), 15–16
Michelangelo, *150*, 151, 156
Mohammed (570?–632), 71, 76, 83

Monasteries,
  destroyed by Henry VIII, 143–7
  life in, 22–5
Montfort, Simon de (1208?–65), 85, 90
More, Thomas (1478–1535), 151, 152, 154, 163
Muslims, 71, 83

Norman Conquest, 50–9
Northumberland, John Dudley, Duke of (1502?–53), 162–3

Ockham, William of (d.1349?), 116
Odo, Bishop of Bayeux (d.1097), 50, *53*
Orleans, Siege of (1429), 123–4, 127
Oswy, King of Northumbria (612?–670), 20

Pagan gods, 18, 45
Parliament,
  called by Simon de Montfort, 85
  called by Edward I, 86
  in Ireland, 88
  managed by Cromwell, 142
  under Elizabeth, 200–2
Paston family, 102–5, 115, 119
Peasants' Revolt (1381), 130–4
Philip Augustus, King of France (1165–1223), 73–6
Philip II of Spain (1556–98), 168, 171, 174, 198
Pilgrimage of Grace (1536), 144, 146
Pilgrims, *65*, 71
Plague (Black Death), 128–9, 134, 187
Polo, Marco (1254?–1324), *82*, 83
Poor Law, 181–2, 194
Poor, in Elizabeth's reign, 179–82
Prayer Book, 162, 166, 196
Printing, 148
Punishments, *30–1*, *96*, 182, 212
Puritans, 200–3

Raleigh, Sir Walter (1552?–1618), *188*, 209–10
Reformation, 158–67
Renaissance, 148–57
Richard I (1157–99), 70, 72–6, *77*, 84
Richard II (1367–1400), 121–2, 131–3, *133*, *134*
Richard III (1452–85), *135*

Ridley, Nicholas, Bishop (1500?–55), 164
Roads, 32, 78
Roman Empire, 12
Russia, 45, 211–12

Saladin, Sultan (1138–93), 72–5
Saxons,
  coming of, 12–17
  conversion of, 18–27
  daily life of, 28–43
  fight against Vikings, 44–9
  Norman Conquest of, 50–9
Schools, *see* Education
Science, 41–2, 115–18, 149
Scotland,
  fight against Edward I, 90–2
  victory over the English, 92
  under Mary, Queen of Scots, 172–3
Servetus, Michael (1511–53), 149
Shakespeare, William (1564–1616), 186–7, 194
Ships, 40, *44–5*, *78*, 204–6
Sieges, 73, *124*
Somerset, Edward Seymour, Duke of (1506?–52), 162, 168
Spenser, Edmund (1552?–99), 171
Sport, 101, *157*, 186, 194
Squires, 98–100
Star Chamber, Court of, 138–9
Sudbury, Simon, Archbishop (d.1381), 131–2
Sutton Hoo treasure, 6, 8–9

Tallis, Thomas (1510?–85), 153
Theatre, 113, 186–7
Three field system, 36, *42*
Torture, 199, *200*
Tournaments, 101, *157*
Tower of London, *168*, *199*
Towns, 6, 36, 39, 110–11, 182–7
Trade, 39–40, 111–13, 182–3, 204
Travel, 40, 78–83, 148, 204–13
Trials, *see* Justice
Turks, 71–5, 148, 212
Tyler, Wat (d.1381), 130–3, *133*
Tyrone, Shane O'Neill, Earl of (1530?–67), 176, *196*

Universities, 114–16
Utopia, 152

Valhalla, 45
Vikings, 44–9
Village settlements, *32*, 32–6, 106–9
Villeins, 57, 85, 106–9
  see also Peasants' Revolt
Virginia, 209, 213
Vortigern (fl.450), 13

Wales,
  settled by Britons, 16
  threatened by Marcher lords, 88–90
  under Edward I, 90, 92
Wallace, Sir William (1272?–1305), 91–2
Walworth, William (d.1385), 132
Wars
  of the Roses, 134–6, 139
  with France, 120–7
  with the Irish, 176
  with the Scots, 90–2
  with Spain, 174–6
  with the Turks, 71–7
  with the Vikings, 44–9
  with the Welsh, 88–90
Warwick, Richard Neville, Earl of (1428–71), 134
Weather forecasting, 116
Wentworth, Peter (1530–96), 201–2, *203*
Whitby, Synod of (664), 20, 26
William I (the Conqueror) (1027–87), 50–8
William II (Rufus) (d.1100), 8–10, *59*, 60
Wine trade, *108*, 120
Witan, 28, *30*
Wolsey Thomas (1475?–1530), 136–41, 147, 161
Women, 33–4, 103–4, 115
Wool trade, 86, 120
Writing, *11*, *24–5*, 25
Wycliffe, John (d.1384), 130

Zwingli, Huldreich (1484–31), 162

Acknowledgements

ILLUSTRATION ACKNOWLEDGEMENTS

Aerofilms Ltd: 7, 15, 98, 102, 145
Ashmolean Museum: 48
Marquess of Bath: 193
Bibliothèque Royale de Belgique:129
Bibliothèque National, Paris: 73, 82, 126
Bodleian Library, Oxford: 68, 91, 101, 113, 128
British Museum: 8, 9, 11, 16, 24, 25, 26, 29, 30, 31, 35, 39, 40, 42, 45, 49, 62, 63, 64, 76, 79, 80,
    84, 85, 86, 96, 99, 100, 103, 104, 105, 106, 108, 109, 110, 112, 113, 116, 118, 119, 122, 124,
    130, 131, 132, 133, 143, 144, 153, 164, 165, 169, 171, 173, 174, 179, 180, 181, 184/185, 199,
    200, 208, 210, 211
British Travel Association: 90
Cambridge University Library: 183
Master and Fellows of Corpus Christi College, Cambridge: 74
Country Life: 114
The Board of Trinity College, Dublin: 111
Chapter Librarian, The College, Durham: 70, 115
Iraq Petroleum Co. Ltd: 75
H. and R. Leacroft, Churches and Cathedrals: 23
London Museum: 65, 103
Master and Fellows of Magdalene College, Cambridge: 205
Manchester Public Libraries: 198
Mansell Collection: 17, 60, 77, 123, 125, 150, 158
Crown copyright, Ministry of Public Building and Works, England: 21, 140, 155, 156
Crown copyright: reproduced by permission of the Ministry of Public Building and Works,
    Scotland: 20
National Maritime Museum: 205, 209
National Monuments Branch, Dublin: 21
National Monuments Record, Crown copyright: 19, 38, 66, 67, 168, 190
National Portrait Gallery: 123, 135, 137, 138, 139, 142, 149, 152, 161, 162, 172, 176, 178, 187,
    189, 206
Universitetes Oldsaksamling: 44, 45
Phaidon Press, The Bayeux Tapestry, ed. Frank Stenton: 51, 52, 53, 54, 55
Public Records Office, Crown copyright: 56, 58, 93, 166
Royal Commission on Historical Monuments, Crown copyright: 71, 87, 140
Marquess of Salisbury: 203
Dr J. K. St Joseph, Selwyn College, Cambridge: 7
Walter Scott (Bradford) Ltd: 12
Edwin Smith, photographer: 57
Society of Antiquaries, London: 95
Sidney Sussex College, Cambridge: 68
Col. N. V. Stopford-Sackville: 163
Trinity College Library, Cambridge: 25, 34, 42, 117
Utrecht University Library: 186
Valentine & Sons Ltd: 92
Victoria and Albert Museum, Crown copyright: 146, 157, 182, 189, 190, 191
Windsor Castle, reproduced by gracious permission of Her Majesty, Queen Elizabeth II: 88, 150

ARTISTS' CREDITS

Gordon Cramp Studio: 13, 14, 27, 46, 61, 72, 89, 112, 121, 175, 207
Dougald Macdougal: 188
Gillian Newing: 46, 97
Edward Poulton: 23, 66/67, 73
Peter Warner: 32, 107
Penguin Education Art Department: 33, 38, 41, 54, 59, 94, 102, 110, 120, 127, 131, 135, 167, 178